Dear Jim,
    As a boy, you're father
was quite a trickster but
we know, in a short time,
you will have him sadly
baffled. Have fun.
        Love
        Pappa & Grandma.

D1458070

Tricks
any boy can do

Tricks
any boy can do

By

Joseph Leeming

HAWTHORN BOOKS, INC., PUBLISHERS

NEW YORK

TRICKS ANY BOY CAN DO

Copyright © 1938 by Joseph Leeming. Copyright under International and Pan-American Copyright Conventions. All rights reserved, including the right to reproduce this book or portions thereof in any form, except for the inclusion of brief quotations in a review. All inquiries should be addressed to Hawthorn Books, Inc., 260 Madison Avenue, New York, New York 10016. This book was manufactured in the United States of America. Library of Congress Catalog Card Number: 38-27215.

17   18   19   20

For

JOSEPH LEEMING, JR.

Foreword

THE tricks described in this book are sufficiently varied and numerous to enable any one interested in magic to entertain and mystify his friends for hours on end. In the selection of the tricks, careful attention has been paid not only to effectiveness and dramatic quality, but also to simplicity of execution. Consequently, even the beginner should have no difficulty in doing all the tricks described. It may be mentioned that to obtain the best tricks of this type, selection has been made from more than two thousand tricks that are available in the world's literature of magic.

It has been truly said that there is a vast difference between telling how a trick is done and teaching how to do it. The reader should bear this in mind and realize that while the present volume tells him how to do a large and diversified number of tricks, he should study at all times to present them with the greatest possible showmanship and éclat. Each performer has a different approach and personality, and each must work out for himself the most suitable method (for him) of presenting his deceptions. It is this study, which cannot be taught by any book, that, added to the information given in books such as the present one, makes of magic an art.

J. L.

Contents

TRICKS WITH CARDS

ix

TRICKS WITH COINS

TRICKS WITH MATCHES AND MATCH BOXES

TRICKS WITH BALLS

TRICKS WITH HANDKERCHIEFS

TRICKS WITH RINGS

TRICKS WITH STRING

TRICKS WITH CIGARETTES AND CIGARS

MIND-READING AND SPIRIT TRICKS

TRICKS WITH NUMBERS

MISCELLANEOUS TRICKS

Tricks with Cards

Making the Pass

ANY one who wishes to do card tricks must sooner or later learn how to locate secretly a card (or cards) which has been selected by the audience. Professional magicians do this by means of a sleight known as the "pass," which brings the chosen card to the top of the deck. As this requires considerable skill and practice, an easier, but just as effective, means of doing the "pass" is described herewith.

When the person is about to return his card, the performer cuts the deck, holding the lower half in his left hand and removing the upper half with his right hand. The spectator then places his card on top of the lower half, and the performer immediately replaces the upper half, but crooks the little finger of his left hand between the two halves of the deck. In this position the deck can be held naturally in the left hand, and it will look as though the two halves have been really reunited.

The next move is the natural one of shuffling the cards. But in shuffling, the performer takes in his right hand all the upper portion of the deck, which is separated from the lower portion by his little finger, and shuffles it back onto the bottom of the cards in the left hand. In this way the chosen card is left on top. No rapid movements are made during the execution of the sleight and there is nothing to excite the suspicions of

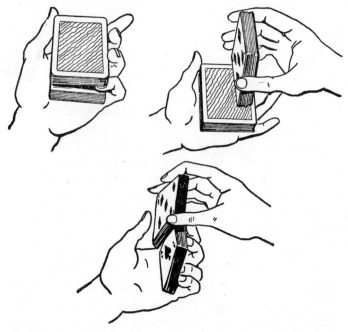

the audience. When the pass is completed, the performer can continue shuffling by using the false shuffle
described below.

Forcing a Card

As with the "pass," the ability to "force" a card,
that is, to make some one select a certain predetermined card, is an invaluable part of the magician's stock

in trade. The professional "force" is very difficult to do, so two simpler methods are described herewith.

The Five-pile Force

THE performer holds a pack of cards face downward and, as he moves his hand across the table, drops a few cards at a time until there are five piles each containing approximately the same number of cards. He then asks a spectator to remove the top card of one of the end piles and place it on the next pile. Another card is removed from the end pile and placed on the second pile away, and two more cards are similarly taken from the end pile and placed on the remaining two piles. The spectator is then asked to look at the top card of the end pile and, after he has memorized it, to gather up the cards and shuffle them together. The performer then tells him the name of the card he has noted, or reveals it in some other way.

This method of forcing a card is accomplished as follows. Before commencing the trick, the performer opens out the cards in his hand with the faces toward him and notes the fifth card from the top. When the five piles have been made, he instructs the spectator to remove the cards from the pile which was previously on top of the deck. Thus, when four cards are taken off and placed on the four other piles, the card on top of the fifth pile is the card that was originally the fifth from the top of the deck and the one the performer memorized before the trick began.

Another Method of Forcing a Card

By alternating this method of forcing with the "Five-pile Force," the magician can do several tricks requiring forced cards in succession, without the audience suspecting that they are being made to select predetermined cards.

In this method, the performer asks a spectator to count off, one by one, any number of cards he desires from the top of a pack, placing them in a pile on the table. The pile is then replaced on the pack and another person is asked to count off the same number of cards, and then to look at the last card dealt and remember it.

This card will, of course, always be the card which was on top of the deck when the first spectator took the cards. The performer simply notes the top card before handing the pack to the spectator, and he then knows in advance precisely what card will be turned over and remembered.

The False Shuffle

ONCE a chosen card has been brought to the top of the
deck by means of the pass, it is always well to shuffle
the cards a few times to give the impression that the

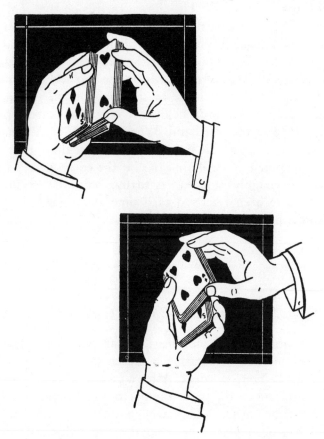

cards are being well mixed. By means of the false
shuffle described herewith, the magician can give the
effect of shuffling the cards thoroughly while at the
same time keeping the chosen card in its place on top
of the deck.

Hold the pack in the left hand with the faces of the
cards toward the left. The chosen card is on top of the
pack. Grip the cards fairly tightly between the left
thumb and fingers. With the right hand, grasp the cards
forming the central portion of the pack and draw them
upwards and clear of the cards on the top and bottom.

Proceed with the shuffle by lowering the right hand
and shuffling the cards held in it onto the bottom of
those held in the left hand. When this has been done,
repeat the false shuffle immediately two or three times.
To the audience it will appear as if the entire pack had
been thoroughly shuffled. Actually, only the middle
cards have been removed each time and shuffled back
onto the bottom of the pack.

Locating a Chosen Card

EVERY magician should be familiar with the "bent
corner" method of locating a chosen card after it has
been shuffled into the deck. After a card has been chosen
and returned to the pack, the performer bends up one
of its inner corners. This may be done just after the
card has been placed between the two halves of the

pack, or the bending can be deferred until the card has been brought to the top by means of the pass.

Once the corner is bent, the cards can be shuffled thoroughly but the chosen card can always be located, by examining the corners of the cards.

One of the most valuable uses of this device is that it enables the performer to bring the chosen card to the top of the pack whenever he wishes to do so. It also makes it possible for the audience to shuffle the pack themselves without the performer losing his ability to find the chosen card after the pack is returned to him.

One of the best ways of revealing a chosen card, when using this method, is to push another card into the pack directly under the bent corner one. The upper cards are turned over and there is the chosen one.

The Telltale Cards

AFTER shuffling the cards, the performer looks through the deck and picks out two cards which, with an air of mystery, he puts in his right-hand coat pocket. He then asks a spectator to choose a card. Immediately this is done, the performer takes the two cards from his pocket, and holding them up, shows that they indicate the chosen suit card by their suit and number.

If, for example, the seven of hearts was chosen, the magician produces from his pocket a seven and a heart.

The trick is done by forcing the card to be chosen. After noting what card the audience will choose, the performer takes two cards from the pack that will reveal the chosen card's suit and number and places these in his pocket. He then forces the proper card, by one of the methods previously described and brings the trick to its startling conclusion as soon as the chosen card has been taken from the deck.

The Turned-over Card

MANY packs of cards have on their backs what are called "one-way" designs, that is, pictures which face one way and are upside down if turned around. The present trick is done with such a pack.

Arrange the cards so the designs on their backs all face in one direction, and ask a spectator to take a card. Before he returns it, turn the pack around, so that when his card is replaced, it will face in the opposite direction to all the others. Shuffle the cards and then deal them one by one, face up, onto the table. When you come to the spectator's card, deal it out without saying anything and deal five or six other cards on top of it. Then stop and say, "I will bet you a dollar that the next card I turn will be your card." The spectator will be sure you have made a mistake, as he has seen his card already dealt. As a consequence, he will accept the bet, or at least tell you that you are dead wrong. When he has poked enough fun at you, quietly draw his card from among those on the table and turn it face down.

Revealing a Thought-of Card

THE magician places the cards on the table and divides them into three equal heaps. He then asks one of the spectators to choose one of the heaps, remove the top card, and place it face down on the table without looking at it.

Picking up the cards, he runs through them and selects two, which he throws on the table. They are, say, a six of clubs and a two of diamonds. The magician says that he believes they indicate the suit and number of the chosen card; that is the six of diamonds. The card on the table is turned over and the magician is found to be correct!

The chosen card is the one which was on top of the pack at the beginning of the trick. The magician runs through the cards and glances at it. He then cuts the pack, first lifting off the top third of the pack and placing it on the table; dropping the next heap to the right and the last heap to the left. This puts the top card, which he knows, on top of the middle heap.

The spectator is asked to select a heap. About eight times out of ten, he will choose the center one. If he does not, but takes one of the end heaps, the performer asks another spectator to choose a heap. If he takes the other end heap, the magician says: "That leaves us one heap. Will some one kindly remove the top card," etc.

If, however, the second person chooses the center heap, the magician at once asks him to remove the top card. The carrying out of the remainder of the trick will cause the audience to forget that the first heap chosen was not the one used.

The Changeable Ace

THE performer looks through the pack and removes the ace of hearts which he holds up for the audience to see. He asks one of the spectators to step forward and hands him the ace, face downward, at the same time throwing a handkerchief over it.

"Let me see," says the performer, "which ace is it that you have in your hand?"

"The ace of hearts," replies the spectator.

"Will you kindly look at it to make sure?" the performer says and removes the handkerchief. The spectator looks at the card and finds that it has changed to the ace of clubs.

This trick is done with the aid of a prepared card. It is made by fastening over the single pip on the ace of clubs a heart cut from another card. The heart pip is held in place by a very small dab of soap. This card, which looks like an ace of hearts except for the index numbers in the corners, is placed in the pack prior to the performance. The performer removes it and, while showing it to the audience, covers the index numbers with his fingers. He then turns it face down and removes the extra pip before giving it to the spectator to hold. If the ace of diamonds is used in place of the ace of clubs, it will not be necessary to be so careful to keep the index numbers covered.

The Secret Card

IN this trick, a spectator picks out a card secretly, while the magician's back is turned. The magician, nevertheless, is able to name the card, or, to give the trick a more elaborate climax, he looks through the pack and withdraws a card which he places in his pocket. The spectator is then asked to look through the pack and discovers that his card is not there. Reaching into his pocket, the magician draws from it the secretly chosen card.

The trick is done as follows. Before doing the trick, the magician looks at the top card. When the pack is given to the spectator, he is asked to count off any number of cards he wishes onto the table, and to tell the magician when he has done so. The top card is now the bottom card of the pile on the table.

The magician then asks that the spectator look at the next card, that is, the top card of those remaining in his hand. This is the secretly chosen card. The cards on the table are then replaced on the pack. The chosen card can be located immediately, as it is the one just beneath the original top card.

Instant Color Change

WHEN neatly executed, this is a very mystifying sleight. The top card of a pack is turned face upwards. It is, say, the three of clubs. The pack is dropped onto the floor and the card is seen to have changed mysteriously to the three of hearts.

The trick is done by air pressure. Before performing it, the three of hearts is placed just below the top card, which is the three of clubs. After the three of clubs has been turned over, both cards are pushed about three-quarters of an inch over the side of the pack.

Now, when the pack is dropped on the floor, the air pressing against the two projecting cards will cause them to turn over, so the three of clubs will land face down and the three of hearts face up.

Finding the Aces

THE magician gives a pack of cards to the audience with the request that they shuffle them thoroughly. When this has been done and the cards are returned, the magician places them in his inside coat pocket. Telling the audience that the aces have a higher vibration than the other cards and that he can consequently detect them because of the sensitiveness of his fingertips, he reaches into his pocket and, one by one, withdraws the four aces.

The trick is simple in the extreme, but like so many other tricks in which some preparation is made, unknown to the audience, the method by which it is accomplished is practically undetectable. In the present instance, the preparation consists of removing the four aces from the pack and placing them in the upper right-hand vest pocket.

After the pack has been shuffled and placed in the coat pocket, the magician reaches in for the aces and withdraws them, one at a time, from their secret hiding place. The fold of the coat makes it impossible for the audience to see that he is actually drawing them from his vest pocket, instead of from his coat pocket, as the audience supposes.

The Card-in-the-glass Vanish

ONE of the spectators chooses a card, which is handed to the performer. He covers it with a handkerchief and allows the audience to feel it through the handkerchief's folds. The card is then placed in a drinking glass and

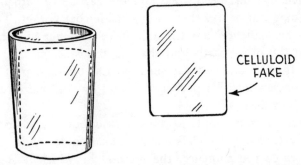

CELLULOID FAKE

for a moment or two it remains there covered by the handkerchief. Then, with a mystic "Pass!" the magician lifts the handkerchief. The card has vanished!

An easily made fake is required for this trick. It is a piece of transparent celluloid cut the size and shape of a playing card. This fake is beneath the handkerchief as it lies on the table at the outset of the trick.

When the chosen card is handed to the performer, he picks up the handkerchief and at the same time pretends to place the card beneath it. Actually, he drops it onto the table, where the rest of the cards have been casu‹ ally spread out. The folds of the handkerchief cover this movement.

The handkerchief and the celluloid fake are then lifted up and several of the spectators are asked to feel the card. The fake is then pushed down into the glass and the trick is carried through to its startling dénouement.

The Adhesive Card

THE "adhesive card" is a very valuable fake which can be used in a number of tricks. It consists of a card, the back of which has been given a light coating of wax or soap. When another card, such as one chosen by a spectator, is placed on top of this card and pressure applied, it adheres to it. The two cards appear as one, and when the pack is gone through, it is discovered the chosen card has vanished.

When using the "adhesive card," place it on the bottom of the pack. If the cards are not pressed together, it will not adhere to the card just above it. After a spectator has chosen a card, slip the "adhesive card" around to the top of the pack. Then place the pack on your left hand and cut it into two portions. When picking up the cards, place the portion with the "adhesive card" on its top, beneath the other portion, and insert the left little finger just above the "adhesive card." Cut the pack again, separating it just above the "adhesive card" and have the spectator replace his card on top of the "adhesive card." With a little practice, the cutting, which is done to get the "adhesive card" into the center of the pack, can be executed very rapidly and naturally.

When the spectator's card has been returned, the performer squares up the pack and presses the cards firmly together. This causes the spectator's card to adhere to the "adhesive card." The cards can then be dealt off, one at a time, and it will be discovered that the spectator's card has disappeared.

The following trick illustrates one way in which the "adhesive card" can be used. The performer removes a card, say the five of diamonds, from another pack and places it in his coat pocket. He then forces the five of diamonds from the pack containing the "adhesive card" on one of the spectators. The spectator returns his card, which is subsequently shown to have disappeared from the pack, and the performer then produces it from his pocket.

All Together

ARRANGE a pack of cards in successive order, that is, place all the clubs together arranged in order from the ace to the king, and arrange the other suits in the same manner. Thus, each suit is separate from the others, and each unit is arranged in numerical, or successive order.

This pack may not be shuffled, but it can be cut, either by the performer or by the audience, as many times as desired. After it has been cut a number of times, deal the cards face down into thirteen piles of four cards each. Pick up the piles and put them together. Then deal off four cards at a time. Each group of four cards will consist of cards of the same value, that is, all the aces will be together, all the two's, and so on.

The Face-up Card

A CARD is chosen from the pack by one of the audience and is returned to the pack. The magician blows upon the cards and starts to deal them one by one onto the table. Unexpectedly, he comes to a card that is face up in the pack. He shows it to the audience and it proves to be the chosen card.

Before doing the trick the performer turns over the bottom card of the pack so it is face up. The cards are then offered to the spectator for him to make his choice, care being taken to keep the upturned bottom card well out of sight beneath the other cards.

While the spectator is looking at his card, the performer turns the pack over so the original bottom card is on top. The chosen card is returned to the pack, which is not fanned out or riffled, but held tightly squared up. Some magicians prefer to take the card from the spectator and replace it in the pack themselves.

The chosen card is now facing in the opposite direction to all the other cards with the single exception of the overturned bottom card. The pack is turned over and the cards are dealt off until the chosen card is discovered face up.

Cutting the Chosen Card

AFTER a card has been chosen and returned to the pack, which is cut a number of times, the performer cuts the pack and, lifting the upper half, reveals the chosen card. It is the bottom card of the upper portion of the deck. The trick may be repeated as often as desired.

The trick is accomplished by means of a so-called "narrow card." This is a card from each side of which a thin strip of about one thirty-second of an inch has been cut off. The difference between this card and the others is so slight that its presence cannot be detected.

In the present trick, after a card has been selected, the magician squares up the pack and taking it by the sides, feels for the slight break caused by the narrow card. He lifts off all the cards above the narrow card, and has the chosen card returned to the pack. Since it is directly on top of the narrow card, it can always be located by cutting the cards as described above.

Counting to the Chosen Card

THIS trick requires the use of two special cards, a narrow one, such as has been described, and a short one, that is, a card from which one thirty-second of an inch has been trimmed from each end.

At the beginning of the trick, the short card is on top of the pack and the narrow card on the bottom. The performer gives the pack to one of the spectators and asks him to count off, one by one, any number of cards he wishes. The spectator, let us assume, counts off twenty-two cards. The short card is now the bottom card of the twenty-two. The spectator is asked to look at it, memorize it, and replace the cards on top of the pack.

The audience may now cut the cards as often as they like, but the first cut will place the narrow card (which was on the bottom of the pack) on top of the twenty-two cards dealt off. It will remain there throughout the cutting.

When the audience have finished cutting the cards, the performer takes them, locates the narrow card, and cuts the pack to bring it to the bottom. He then asks the spectator how many cards he counted. Twenty-two. The performer counts off twenty-two cards and turns over the last one. It is the short card and the one that was memorized by the spectator.

The Chosen Suit

THE magician asks that some one select one of the suits of a pack of cards: clubs, hearts, diamonds, or spades, and write on a piece of paper, "Which suit is it?" While this is being done, the magician leaves the room. His assistant then brings him the pencil and paper, and the magician at once writes down the name of the suit selected by the spectator.

The trick is done by using four different pencils, each one identifying a particular suit. Thus, for example, a long yellow one might mean clubs, a short yellow one, hearts, a long red one, spades and a short blue one, diamonds. The assistant has these in his pocket and as soon as a suit is chosen, he gives the corresponding pencil to the spectator with which to write his question. The same pencil is then carried out to the magician and tells him at once which suit was chosen.

Face to Face

A CARD is chosen and returned to the pack. The performer then draws a card and pushes it face up into the pack. Upon going through the cards until the face-up one is come to, it is discovered that the chosen card is just above it, face to face with it.

This trick depends upon the use of the "narrow

card" described in a previous trick. The chosen card is replaced on top of the narrow card. The cards are then cut a few times, a card is withdrawn and, feeling with his finger tips for the narrow card, the performer separates the pack slightly at this point and puts his card in the pack face up, directly on top of the narrow card.

The Upturned Card

A SPECTATOR chooses a card, and it is returned to the pack. The performer then asks at what number from the top the audience would like the chosen card to appear. The cards are counted off, but the chosen card is not at the appointed number. The magician, however, hands the pack to a spectator and asks him to count off the proper number of cards. The spectator does so and there, surprisingly, is the chosen card, face up in the pack.

The chosen card is first brought to the top of the pack. The audience then chooses where they wish it to appear, say ninth from the top. The performer deals eight cards one by one onto the table, which he then picks up and holds in his hand. The ninth card is then dealt off onto the table.

While the audience is looking at it to see if it is the chosen one, the performer returns the other cards to the top of the pack. As he does so, he turns over the bottom card of the eight. This card is the chosen one,

for it was on top of the pack when the dealing com-
menced and was thus the first card placed on the table.
Hence it is the bottom card of the eight which the performer picked up.

As soon as the audience have announced that the
ninth card is not the chosen card, the performer asks
that it be placed on the top of the pack. One of the
spectators is then asked to count off nine cards and
when he does so, the chosen card is, of course, the ninth
one and is face up in the pack.

The Traveling Two

THIS trick is similar to several older tricks, in which
cards inserted in different parts of the pack reappear at
unexpected places, but it employs a different principle.
The effect is that a two of clubs (or of any other suit)
is placed in the center of the pack; the cards are riffled,
and at the magician's always potent command "Pass,"
the two is discovered on the top of the pack.

Before doing the trick, the two of clubs is placed on
top of the pack. The performer then looks through the
cards until he locates the three of clubs. He takes this
card from the pack, covering the center pip with his
thumb, as he does so, and exhibits it to the audience as
the two. Naturally, the card is not held stationary, but
is moved from left to right once or twice so all can see
it, and the continuous motion makes it impossible for

the audience to detect the fact that it is not really the two.

The three is then placed on top of the pack and the performer immediately picks it up and places it in the center of the pack. The cards are riffled and the top card, the real two of clubs, is removed and shown to the audience.

Card Subtraction

HANDING a pack of cards to one of the audience, the magician asks him to place any five spot-cards (that is, not court-cards) in a row and to add the total of their spots. Suppose they total 23, as shown in the illustrative example given below. The performer asks that the spectator draw from the pack two cards whose values are the same as the figures in the total. In this case, a 2 and a 3 are required. These are placed beneath the two right-hand cards of the first row.

The spectator is now asked to subtract these two cards from the cards above them. This gives a 5 and a 2, which are placed at the bottom of the two right-hand rows. To the left of them are placed three other cards which are of the same values as those directly above them in the first row.

The magician now turns his back and asks the spectator to remove any card in the bottom row, and when he has done so to add up the spots on the remaining cards.

When he has done this and announced the total, the performer immediately tells him what card was removed.

The value of the chosen card is easily determined by subtracting the total of the remaining cards from the next higher multiple of 9. Thus, in the example given below, if the three were removed, the total of the remaining cards (6-2-2-5) is 15. Subtract this from 18, the next higher multiple of 9, and the remainder is 3, the value of the chosen card.

The following example shows how the cards are to be laid out:

$$6—3—2—4—8 = 23$$
$$2—3$$
$$6—3—2—2—5$$

The Inseparable Suits

THE magician removes the twelve court-cards from a pack of cards and lays them on the table in three rows, each row containing four cards. He then gathers them up and cuts them several times, after which he deals them into four separate piles. Although the cards appear to have been thoroughly mixed, it is discovered, when the four piles are turned over, that the three cards of each suit have gotten together, for each pile contains a separate suit.

To do the trick. the cards are placed on the table

in the following manner. In the first row of four cards, put four cards of different suits—one heart, one club, one diamond, and one spade.

Make the first card of the second row of the same suit as the last card in the first row. Make the second card of the same suit as the first card in the first row; the third card of the same suit as the second card in the first row, and the fourth card of the same suit as the third card in the first row.

The first card of the third row is of the same suit as the last card in the second row; the second card is of the same suit as the first card in the second row, and so on, the cards in the third row being arranged in relation to those in the second row, as those in the second row were to those in the first.

The following example makes the method of arrangement clear:

Heart	Club	Diamond	Spade
Spade	Heart	Club	Diamond
Diamond	Spade	Heart	Club

The cards are picked up in vertical rows, placing the last card in the third row on the last card of the second row and putting both these cards on the last card of the first row. The other rows are picked up in a like manner, and the cards can then be cut as often as desired without altering their arrangement as to suits.

The Twenty Cards

THE magician deals ten pairs of cards onto the table, twenty cards in all. He then asks several members of the audience to select and memorize any of the pairs they wish to, without letting him know what cards they choose. The cards are then gathered up and redealt and the magician tells each spectator what two cards he selected.

When the cards are dealt the second time, they are placed on the table in accordance with an arrangement based on the following four words:

COLOR
SHEER
USUAL
CHAFF

The first card of the first pair is placed on the C of the word *color;* and the second card of the pair on the C in the word *chaff.* The first card of the second pair is placed on the first O of *color,* and the second card on the second O of *color.*

The next pair is placed on the two L's in *color* and *usual;* the next on the two R's in *color* and *sheer,* and so on. In the four words there are just ten pairs of two letters, so each pair corresponds in position to the position of the two letters.

To discover the spectators' cards, ask them what row, or rows, his cards are in. If he says rows 1 and 4, they are the two cards on the two letters C. If in rows

2 and 3, they are on the two S's; if both are in row 3, they are on the two U's in *usual,* and so on.

The Card in the Pocket

THE magician asks one of the spectators to memorize a card as he ruffles the deck, and to write the name of the chosen card on a piece of paper. Handing the pack to another member of the audience, the magician asks that the name of the chosen card be read aloud. The spectator holding the pack is asked to look through it and finds that the chosen card has disappeared. Without more ado, the magician produces it from his pocket.

The entire deck is not shown to the audience, when the selection is being made, but only the top ten cards. These, the magician has arranged and memorized before showing the trick. One of the easiest ways to memorize a series of cards like this is to arrange them so that each card is three higher than the preceding one. For example, start with a three, then six, nine, queen, two, five, eight, Jack, ace, and four.

As soon as the spectator has chosen his card from among the ten top ones, the magician asks him to write its name on a piece of paper. This gives him an excuse to turn his back and, as he does so, he removes the top ten cards and places them in one of his waistcoat pockets. The entire movement is easily hidden from the spectators. As soon as the name of the chosen card is announced, the magician removes it from his pocket, being able to locate it directly, as he has memorized the order of the cards.

Picking the Court-cards

ALL the court-cards are removed from the pack and thoroughly shuffled by one of the audience. The magician then takes the cards and holding them behind his back produces them one at a time, telling the audience in advance whether the card is a jack, a king, or a queen.

A few moments work with a jack-knife prepares the ground for this trick. Run the knife along the sides of each king so as to roughen the edges, and do the same with the ends of each queen. The jacks are left unprepared.

When this has been done, the cards are returned to the pack, but after they have been removed, they can easily be identified without being seen, by simply running fingers along their edges.

Separating the Colors

THE performer shuffles a pack of cards thoroughly and then, despite the fact that the two colors, red and black, have been inextricably intermingled, he proceeds to deal the cards into two piles, one of which is found to contain all the red cards, and the other all the black cards.

This exceptionally startling effect is obtained with the aid of nothing more than a common pin. With it the magician prepares a pack of cards by punching a small hole from the front of the card to the back near the lower left-hand corner of each red card. When this has been done, the red cards are put back in the pack, with the corners in which the holes have been made all on the right-hand side and on the edge of the pack nearest the performer as he holds the cards in his hand.

It is very easy to feel the holes with the thumb as the cards are being dealt and thus be sure that all the punched cards go into one pile and the unprepared cards into the other pile.

The Cards in the Pocket

THE performer places a pack of cards in one of his coat pockets and then asks one of the audience to draw a card from another pack. As soon as this has been done, he puts his hand in his coat pocket and withdraws three cards which, by their number and suit, reveal the identity of the chosen card.

If, for example, the chosen card is the nine of hearts, the magician first withdraws a heart to indicate the suit, and then brings out two other cards whose spots total nine.

All that is needed to reveal by this method any card in the entire pack is four cards. They are:

Ace of hearts	Three of diamonds
Two of spades	Seven of clubs

These cards are placed in order on top of the deck, the ace on top, the two next, and so on, before the pack is placed in the magician's pocket, so it is an easy matter for him to withdraw any of them that he wishes to.

With a little practice, the various combinations which are necessary to disclose any card, are soon learned. Always reveal the suit first, adding whatever other cards are needed afterwards.

The Telephone Trick

THIS trick is one of the best of all "parlor" card tricks and the person who prepares for it beforehand can always be sure of mystifying any one with whom he happens to be spending the evening or a formal audience.

The performer gives a pack of cards to one of the audience and asks him to select a card. Another person is then asked to go to the telephone and call a number which the performer gives him. The person who answers the phone is asked to name the chosen card, which he does without hesitation.

The person on the other end of the phone is, of course, a confederate, but even though the audience knows or suspects this they will never be able to find out how he knows the chosen card. Actually, he is apprized of the name of the card by the name by which he is called when he answers the phone. This name is given the person making the call by the magician.

The number of the card is represented by the first name and the suit is represented by the last name. To denote an ace, a first name beginning with A, such as Allen or Arthur, is used. To denote a two, use a first name beginning with B, such as Bob or Bill, and so on through the rest of the pack. A convenient list is given herewith:

Ace .... (A)llen		Eight ...... (H)erbert
Two .... (B)ob		Nine ..... (I)saac
Three ...... (C)harlie		Ten ...... (J)ames
Four .... (D)an		Jack ...... (K)ing
Five .... (E)dward		Queen .... (L)awrence
Six .... (F)rank		King ...... (M)artin
Seven ...... (G)us			

The suits are denoted by the first letter of the person's last name, as follows:

Clubs ..... (A)bbott	Spades .... (C)arlson
Hearts .... (B)enedict	Diamonds .. (D)rew

By this system, the ace of clubs, for example, would be indicated by such a name as Allen Abbott: the jack of spades would be King Carlson, and so on.

By having several friends acting as confederates, each one equipped with a small card bearing the code, the trick can be performed at any time and can be repeated several times in rapid succession, a different phone number being used each time.

The Card in the Bowl

THE performer asks one of the spectators to choose a card and return it to the pack. When this has been done, he shows the audience an ordinary dinner plate and china bowl. Placing the plate upon the bowl, he puts the cards on the plate. Waving his wand and uttering a magic word, the magician orders the chosen card to pass through the plate and into the bowl. Upon looking through the pack it is found that it has disappeared, and when the plate is removed, it is found reposing in the bowl.

The secret, as in the case of some other effective bits of magic, lies in the use of a small dab of soap. This is pressed against the bottom of the plate before the performance.

When the chosen card is returned to the pack, it is brought to the top of the pack by means of the pass and kept there while the pack is shuffled by means of the false shuffle. The cards are then placed on the table and the magician exhibits the plate to the audience. After showing it back and front, he places it on top of

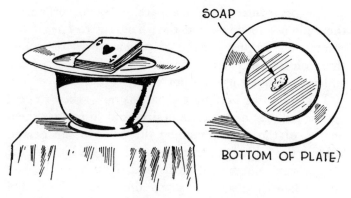

SOAP

BOTTOM OF PLATE)

the cards, at the same time picking up the bowl and showing it to the audience.

The chosen card naturally adheres to the soap on the bottom of the plate and comes with the plate when it is lifted and placed over the bowl. The easiest way to dislodge the chosen card is to do so by means of the fingers just as the plate is being placed on the bowl. If the plate is held with the thumb on top and the fingers underneath and is tilted towards the audience while it is being placed in position, this will be found very simple to accomplish.

Telling a Card Dealt by a Spectator

THIS trick, which is a combination of several basic principles of magic, is exceptionally baffling and has the added merit of requiring no sleight of hand whatever.

The performer shuffles a pack of cards, or allows the audience to do so and then hands it to one of the spectators. Taking a piece of paper, he writes something on it, folds it and hands it to a member of the audience, requesting him not to look at it.

The spectator holding the pack is now asked to deal off any number of cards he desires and to replace them on top of the pack. Handing the pack to the person holding the folded paper, the magician asks him to deal off the same number of cards and to turn up the last one. When this has been done, the paper is unfolded and is found to contain the name of the card which has been turned up.

The magician knows, well in advance, the name of the card which will be turned up, because it is the card on top of the pack when he gives it to the first person to deal. While holding the cards in his hands with their faces toward him, he quietly notes the top card and writes its name on the piece of paper.

When the first person deals his cards, the top card automatically becomes the bottom card of the pile dealt off, as it is the first card to be placed on the table. Consequently, when the second spectator deals the same number of cards, the last card, which he turns over, is bound to be the one whose name was written on the paper.

Odd and Even

THE magician cuts a pack of cards into two equal halves and placing one half on the table, asks a member of the audience to draw a card from the other half. When the spectator has noted his card, the magician asks him to replace it himself in the half of the deck which is on the table and to shuffle the cards thoroughly.

Although the performer has not touched the cards in any way and has, therefore, had absolutely no opportunity of knowing which is the chosen card, he finds it at once upon looking through the cards.

The secret lies in the fact that before showing the trick, the performer separates the pack into two halves, one containing all the even cards and the other all the odd cards. By slightly bending, or curving, one half before placing it on top of the other, it is easy to cut the pack at the right place to separate the two halves.

The chosen card is, of course, detected without difficulty, as it is the only odd or even one, as the case may be, in the half of the pack into which it has been shuffled.

Naming the Cards

THIS is an ingenious method of arranging a pack of cards, so that every card in the pack can be named, as they are dealt off one by one. To give variation to the trick, and also to keep the audience from suspecting that the cards have been prearranged, it is often advisable to deal the cards one by one face down, and ask the audience to call "Stop" when they want a card named. The magician will always be able to give the name of the card, and to verify his announcement by turning the card over.

The pack is arranged in a sequence which is indicated by the following bit of doggerel:

> Eight kings threatened to save
> Ninety-five ladies for one sick knave.

Translated, this means:

> Eight-king-three-ten-two-seven
> Nine-five-queen-four-ace-six-jack.

This is the order in which the cards are arranged by number. By suits they are arranged—clubs, hearts, spades, diamonds.

To arrange the pack, lay the eight of clubs face up on the table. Upon it place the king of hearts; then the three of spades; then the ten of diamonds; then the two of clubs, and so on. The suits always go clubs, hearts, spades, diamonds, and the number always follows the numbers indicated by the verse.

With very little practice, you will be able to follow the cards perfectly, as you deal them off the pack, repeating the doggerel as the dealing proceeds.

The Card on the Wall

THIS is a good surprise finish to a trick in which one of the spectators has chosen a card, which the magician wishes to reveal in a startling way.

The chosen card is brought to the top of the pack by means of the pass. As soon as it is in this position, a small bit of soap or wax, which has been made ready beforehand and placed in a convenient position on the table, is affixed to it. Standing quite close to the wall, the magician throws the pack against the wall. The impact is sufficient to make the wax on the back of the chosen card adhere to the wall and hold the chosen card there, while the rest of the pack falls to the floor.

The Card Clock

THE magician puts twelve cards, face down, on the table, arranging them in a circle, as though they were the twelve numbers on the face of a clock. He then asks that, while his back is turned, one of the spectators will pick up one of the cards and memorize it, as well as what number it corresponds to on the clock.

When the card has been replaced, the magician gathers up all twelve and puts them in his pocket, immediately thereafter removing eleven cards and throwing them on the table. The audience is asked to look through these to see if the chosen card is among them. It is not there and the magician produces it from his pocket!

Before showing the trick, the performer puts eleven cards in his pocket. In gathering up the twelve cards from the table, care is taken to pick them up in order, starting with the card corresponding to one o'clock and finishing with the card representing twelve o'clock.

The twelve cards are placed in the same pocket as that which already contains the eleven cards, but are kept separated from them. The eleven cards are thrown on the table, and after the audience has looked through them without finding the selected card, the performer asks what number, or time of day, the chosen card corresponded to. When the answer is given he says, "Ah, I thought so," and counting down to the right card among the twelve in his pocket, he produces the chosen card.

The Transferred Cards

PLACING a pack of cards on the table, the magician asks a spectator to cut them and place either half of the pack he chooses in one of his pockets. The magician then counts the remaining cards and tells the audience their number. Suppose there are thirty-two; this makes the number of cards in the spectator's pocket twenty.

The magician puts his cards in one of his pockets,

utters the magic word "Pass," and announces that he has made four cards fly from the spectator's pocket to his own. Upon counting the two heaps of cards, it is found that the spectator has only sixteen, while the performer has thirty-six.

The trick is done by concealing four cards in the pocket before commencing the performance. The audience, not knowing that this has been done, naturally assumes that the spectator has all the cards with the exception of those held by the performer, for the spectator does not actually count his own cards.

Duplicating the Count

ONE of the spectators is given a pack of cards and asked to take as many cards as he wants from the top of the pack. The cards are to be taken in one group, at one time, that is, without counting them off one by one.

The magician then asks the spectator to count the cards he has removed, without letting him know how many there are. The cards are then replaced in the pack, and the magician immediately counts off the same number as were taken by the spectator.

The trick is done by the simple method of bending the cards left in the magician's hand. This can be done unobserved by holding the cards endwise between the thumb and fingers and bending up the ends.

After the spectator's cards have been replaced, there

will be a slight space between them and the rest of the pack, which indicates to the performer when he has dealt off all the spectator's cards.

The "Stop" Trick

THE magician deals the cards one by one on the table and asks a spectator to tell him when to stop. When the spectator says "Stop," the magician asks him to turn over the last card dealt, memorize it, and replace it.

He then places the remaining cards on the pack and deals the cards out into four piles of thirteen cards each. The spectator is asked to gather these up and then deal them out one by one. At a certain point, the magician, in his turn, says "Stop." The last card dealt is turned over and is found to be the spectator's card.

This trick depends upon careful counting. As the cards are dealt the first time, count each one, so that when the spectator says "Stop," you will know what number his card is from the bottom. Suppose it is number 31. This means that when the remaining twenty-one cards are put on the pack, the chosen card will be the twenty-second from the top of the pack.

Now deal the cards into four heaps and note in which heap and in what position in the heap the chosen card comes. It is then easy to know just where it will be when the four heaps have been gathered up, by noting carefully, the order in which they are picked up.

Suppose, for example, that the heap containing the chosen card was the third to be picked up and that the chosen card is the third from the top of the heap. This will make it the sixteenth card from the top of the pack, as each heap contains thirteen cards, and only one heap was placed on top of the one containing the chosen card.

The Lightning Change

THE magician holds up a card and, after every one present has seen it, throws it on the floor and asks one of the spectators to put his foot on top of it. In a moment, he asks the spectator to retrieve the card just to make sure it is the right one. To everybody's astonishment, it has changed into an entirely different card.

When the first card is shown to the audience, another card is in back of it. The two cards are held with the fingers at the back and the thumb in front. (This is important). When the card is thrown to the floor, the fingers push the back card forward and it falls to the floor face downwards. As part of the same motion the thumb is drawn inward, pushing the front card into the palm of the hand. It is concealed here for a moment until the performer asks the spectator to look at the card under his foot, when, with everybody's eyes looking toward the spectator, it is an easy matter to replace it undetected on the top of the pack.

Tricks with Coins

The Folded-paper Coin Vanish

THIS is an excellent method of vanishing a coin and one which requires practically no sleight of hand. It can be used in connection with any coin trick involving the disappearance and later discovery of a coin.

The coin is placed in the center of a square piece of paper. The right-hand side of the paper is folded over so as to cover the coin, the crease being made at a point distant one-third of the paper's width from the right-hand edge. The left-hand edge is then folded over in the same manner. This forms a narrow tube with the coin inside.

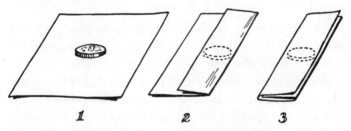

1   *2*   *3*

The magician picks up the tube with his right hand, the fingers closing over the coin. He then transfers it to his left hand, tilting it as he does so, thus allowing the coin to slip out into his left hand. Immediately this is done, he grasps the bottom of the tube between his left thumb and fingers, and holds it this way while, with his right hand, he folds over the top third of the tube. The paper is then reversed and the right hand folds over the opposite end.

The coin is now safely hidden in the left hand, though the audience supposes it to be safely wrapped up in the paper.

The Handkerchief Coin Vanish

THIS is one of the best and simplest methods by means of which a coin can be vanished without the use of sleight of hand. A handkerchief is prepared by placing a coin in one corner and sewing over it a piece of material similar to that of which the handkerchief is made.

The coin to be vanished is placed in the center of the prepared handkerchief and apparently wrapped up, but in reality the sewed-in coin is enfolded, and the real coin is retained in the performer's hand. When the handkerchief is later shaken out, the coin is found to have disappeared for the sewed-in coin is, of course, invisible.

The Coin "Pull"

THIS little device is another useful one for the magician who wishes to have more than one way to make a coin disappear. It consists of a thin piece of metal (an identification disk is ideal) to which a piece of cord elastic is attached. A safety-pin is fastened to the other end of the elastic, which runs up the right sleeve, and is fastened so that the disk hangs down inside the shirt cuff.

A bit of soap is smeared on one side of the disk. When about to vanish a coin, the disk is gotten, unobserved, into the right hand. The coin is held in the left hand and shown to the audience. It is then placed on the right palm on top of the disk to which it adheres. The right hand is then closed, and the right arm is extended as if the coin were being tossed away. This motion snaps the disk up the right sleeve, and the hand is immediately opened and shown to be empty.

A Good Coin-vanishing Box

THE box described herewith will be found a very useful piece of apparatus, for with its aid, a coin can be vanished without the aid of sleight of hand of any kind.

The box is of the cylindrical type in which adhesive tape is sold. It is painted dead black inside and, for the sake of contrast it is well to paint it a bright red on the outside. The coin, either a penny or a dime, which is used with this box, is painted black on one side.

The unpainted side of the coin is shown the audience, but when it is placed in the box, it is dropped so the painted side is uppermost. When the box is opened, the coin has apparently disappeared, as the black side of the coin matches the inside coloring of the box.

The Coin Box

A VERY useful box which can be used either to appear or to vanish a coin can be easily made from a round pill-box.

The box is prepared by separating the middle section, or collar, from the bottom to which it was originally glued. When this has been done, the box is reversible, that is, either the top or bottom can be

removed at the magician's pleasure, by simply turning the box over.

To cause a coin to appear in the box, it is fastened
to the inside of the top with a bit of soap. The top is
removed and the box shown empty. After the cover has
been replaced a slight shake will dislodge the coin,
and upon opening the box, it is revealed to the audience.

To vanish a coin, a bit of soap is fastened to the
inside of the bottom. The coin is pressed against the
soap so it will adhere to it. After the top has been put
on, the magician turns the box over, and when opening it, removes the portion that was originally the
bottom.

The Coin Pass
(Le Tourniquet)

IN a number of tricks it is necessary for the performer
to pretend to transfer a coin from one hand to the
other, though actually retaining it in the original hand.
The pass here described, known to professional magicians as the "tourniquet," is the best way to carry out
this sleight.

The coin is held between the thumb and first and
second fingers of, say, the left hand, the palm of the
hand being upward. The right thumb is passed under
the coin and the right fingers above it. The fingers
and thumb are brought together just as though inclos-
ing the coin. At this moment the coin is released and

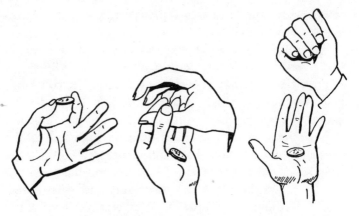

allowed to drop into the palm of the left hand. The right hand, closed as if holding the coin, is drawn away and the performer follows it with his eyes to keep the attention of the audience focused upon it. The coin is retained in the left hand, if the trick requires this to be done, or is unobtrusively placed on the magician's table. In the latter case, the left hand is immediately shown to be empty.

The Disappearing Dime

THE magician places a dime between two half-dollars which are held at the tips of the right thumb and fore-finger. One of the half-dollars is dropped into the left hand and then the other. Opening his right hand the magician shows that the dime has vanished.

The half-dollars are then spun in the air, one after the other and are replaced, one on top of the other, in the right hand. Pass! They are separated and the dime is found to be between them.

The trick is done with the aid of one of the magician's most trusted friends—a small dab of soap. This is smeared on one side of one of the half-dollars.

In doing the trick, the unsoaped half-dollar is held between the thumb and forefinger of the right hand and the dime is placed upon it. The other half-dollar is then placed, soap side down, on top of the dime, to which it adheres.

The dime and half-dollar are then dropped into the left hand, the dime remaining underneath and therefore out of sight. The other half-dollar follows and the right hand is shown empty.

The right hand then picks up the plain half-dollar, spins it in the air, and replaces it in his left hand. The dime and half-dollar are then spun in a like manner and caught in the right hand. The weight of the dime will cause it to fall with the dime underneath.

Both hands are held out to show that they contain only the two half-dollars, one in each hand. The left hand then takes its half-dollar in the fingertips and places it on top of the half-dollar in the right hand. As this is done, however, the half-dollar in the right hand is turned over, by tilting the palm of the hand, thus bringing the dime uppermost and between the two half-dollars. This movement is covered by the approach of the left hand and can even be aided by the left thumb.

Presto! the uppermost half-dollar is lifted and there is the dime. It is picked up and exhibited and all three coins are thrown on the table.

The Coin in the Glass

THIS is an exceptionally clever deception and one which the magician will find very useful as a means of vanishing a coin.

The magician places the coin that is to be vanished in the center of a handkerchief. Then he takes a small glass in his left hand and, picking up the coin and the handkerchief, places the coin over the glass, with the folds of the handkerchief hanging down and concealing it from the view of the audience. He drops the coin into the glass and everybody hears it tinkle, as he does so.

When the handkerchief is removed from the glass, however, the coin has disappeared.

Actually, the coin is never dropped into the glass at all. It is dropped against the side of the glass and this contact makes exactly the same sound as if it dropped right into the glass. After striking the side of the glass, the coin drops down into the fingers of the left hand, and the coin is kept concealed in this hand as long as is required. The attention of the audience is diverted from the left hand, by the magician lifting the covered glass with his right hand and placing it on a table where it remains until such time as he is ready to remove the handkerchief and disclose the coin's disappearance.

Melting Money

THIS trick can be done at any time as it requires no apparatus or preparation. The performer holds out his closed right hand and shakes it so the audience can hear some coins clinking inside it. Asking one of the spectators to hold his wrist so the coins will not be able to disappear up his sleeve, he suddenly says "Pass" and opens his right hand. The coins have vanished completely.

The trick is done by secreting several coins in the left hand. When the right hand is held out, closed as though it held the coins, it is really empty. The magician, however, holds his right wrist with his left hand and, as he shakes his hand, it sounds as though the clinking coins were in his right hand.

To make the act of holding the right wrist with the left hand plausible, the magician must introduce the trick by telling one of the spectators that he wants him to hold his wrist "just this way," suiting the action to the words, explaining that this precaution is taken to eliminate the possibility of the coins being pulled up his sleeve by an elastic band.

The Coin Through the Table

THE magician places a coin on the table and places a tumbler over it, covering the tumbler with a large handkerchief. He then holds another tumbler under the table and utters the word "Pass." Immediately, the coin is heard to rattle into the glass under the table. Upon removing the handkerchief, it is discovered that the coin on the table has vanished.

WHITE PAPER

This trick makes use of an old fake, namely, a tumbler with a piece of white paper pasted over its mouth. The coin on the table is placed on a sheet of white paper which matches the paper affixed to the tumbler. When the tumbler is placed on the coin, the paper hides it. To prevent the audience from seeing that it has disappeared, the handkerchief is placed over the glass at the same time that the glass is placed over the coin.

The coin which falls into the glass held beneath the table is a duplicate which has been attached to the under side of the table with a bit of soap prior to showing the trick. It is released at the proper moment by pushing the edge of the glass against it.

Multiplying Coins

THIS is an excellent version of the favorite multiplying-coins trick which has the virtue of being new and little known.

Three pennies are borrowed from the audience and placed in the performer's right hand. Tossing them into his left hand, he shows that there are still three pennies only. After tossing them back and forth several times, the magician keeps them in his left hand, which he closes and asks the audience how many pennies he has. Although it is obvious to every one that there are only three, the magician has fooled them again and when he opens his hand, there are four pennies in it.

Four pennies are used for the trick. One of them is placed in the left hand before the commencement of the trick, being nipped between the first and second fingers. When the three pennies borrowed from the audience are placed in the right hand, one of them is also placed between the fingers in the same way, so that it can be held onto or released at the performer's pleasure. The other two pennies are held loose in the right palm.

In tossing the (presumably) three pennies from hand to hand, only two are actually tossed each time. Thus, there are always three pennies to be shown the audience in the hand that has just received the two.

Whenever the performer is ready to bring the trick to its dénouement, he really throws three pennies, instead of two, thus bringing all four pennies together in one hand.

The Penetrating Coin

IN this trick a coin passes right through a handkerchief held by one of the spectators. The coin is held in the performer's left hand and is covered with the handkerchief which is then given to a spectator to hold. Even though covered, the round shape of the coin can be clearly seen.

The magician then places another handkerchief over the person's fist. At the mystic word "Pass," he re-moves it and reveals the coin lying on top of the handkerchief it was wrapped up in, having penetrated right through the cloth.

The secret of the trick lies in the use of a piece of thin copper wire bent into the shape of a circle the size of a quarter, or whatever coin is to be used. This fake is held in the left hand and is substituted for the coin when the handkerchief is thrown over the performer's left hand.

The coin is transferred to the right hand and when the second handkerchief is thrown over the spectator's hand, the performer puts his right hand underneath it "to pull the coin through." Grasping the wire, the ends of which are not twisted together, he pulls one end through the handkerchief. This done, he releases the coin held in his right hand so that it will be in its proper position on top of the underneath handkerchief and then removes the upper handkerchief. The wire is removed by the right hand and secreted at the first opportunity.

The Magnetic Coin

THIS is quite a mystifying little effect which will even surprise the magician himself the first time he tries it. It seems almost impossible and yet it works every time.

In effect, the magician passes his hands over a coin and magnetizes it by this time-honored magical procedure. This done, he places it against his forehead where it remains as though it really had been magnetized.

The coin is made to stick by simply placing it against the forehead and pushing it upwards, at the same time pressing it hard against the forehead. After the trick is finished, pass the coin for inspection to show that no glue or other adhesive has been used.

The Coin in the Handkerchief

THIS is an excellent way to produce a coin, from nowhere, which is one thing a magician is always supposed to be able to do.

The performer takes a handkerchief and shows it back and front to demonstrate that it is unprepared and has nothing hidden in it. He then rolls it up into a ball and hands it to one of the audience. Upon unrolling it, a dime is found inside.

 The best type of handkerchief to use is a bandana with a wide border such as can be obtained at any ten-cent store. A few stitches are removed from one side of the border, leaving a small recess in which the dime is placed. When exhibiting the handkerchief before the trick, the side with the dime in it is at the bottom, so the dime will not fall out. In rolling up the

handkerchief, the performer makes sure that the dime emerges from its hiding place so it will be in full view when the handkerchief is opened up.

Flying Money

BEFORE doing this trick, the magician conceals three pennies in his right hand. He then borrows twelve additional pennies from the audience which are counted out onto the table.

One of the audience is asked to pick up three pennies and hold them tightly in his hand. The magician then takes the remaining pennies and gives them to another spectator, dropping them into his hand and at the same time dropping the three pennies concealed in his right hand. Thus, when he closes his hand, he actually holds twelve pennies instead of nine, as he supposes.

The magician takes the three pennies from the first spectator and by means of the "Coin Pass" causes them to vanish. (If the "Coin Pass" is not used, the coins may be vanished by one of the other methods described in this volume.) The second spectator is then asked to open his hand and count his pennies. The three vanished ones have flown invisibly into his hand, giving him twelve instead of the nine that he thought he had.

The Shrinking Half-dollar

TAKING a quarter, the magician places it in the center of a piece of note-paper and draws around it with a pencil, so that there is a circle just the size of a quarter drawn on the paper. The circle is cut out with a pair of scissors, and the magician tells the audience that he is able to pass a half-dollar through this hole. The feat appears to be impossible, but, as usual, the magician carries out his promise and accomplishes the seemingly impossible.

HOLE

HALF DOLLAR

The trick is done by folding the paper over so that the line of the crease passes through the center of the hole. The half-dollar is then placed in the fold directly over the hole and the ends of the paper are pulled upwards and inwards. This elongates the hole sufficiently to allow the half-dollar to slip through it without difficulty.

The Coin under the Cards

THE magician lays a coin on the table and places two playing cards on top of it. A match box is then put on top of the cards. The magician grasps the uppermost card and slides it, together with the match box, across the table to the left until it is a foot or so away from

the other card, beneath which is the coin. He picks up another match box and places it on the card covering the coin. Pass! The match boxes are removed and then the cards. The coin has vanished from its original place and has flown invisibly to beneath the left-hand card.

The secret lies in the fact that the coin is attached

to the first match box by means of a hair or a very
fine piece of black thread. The hair, or thread, is fastened with soap, or glue, to the under sides of both
the box and the coin. It will not be long, but will be
long enough so the coin can be lifted from the table
and shown the audience.

The two cards are placed over the coin, their ends
pointing to left and right. The attached match box
is then placed on top of them. Thus, the hair, or
thread, runs from the coin, around the left ends of the
cards and to the under side of the match box on top
of the cards.

The performer grasps the upper card and slides it
to the left. Naturally, the end of the card pushes
against the hair, or thread, and the coin is pulled along
beneath the card. The other match box is then placed
on the remaining card, the magician gives the command "Pass!" and the mysterious flight of the coin
is revealed.

The Coin in the Hat

A COIN is borrowed from the audience and marked
with a pencil so it can be identified. It is then dropped
into a hat in which a number of other coins of the same
value have previously been placed. The magician
reaches into the hat, and immediately picks out the
marked coin from among the others.

The trick requires a somewhat delicate sense of touch, but can be done by practically anybody. The marked coin is passed among the members of the audience, prior to being dropped into the hat, the excuse for this being that every one may know what the mark looks like. During this process, the spectators' hands warm the coin and it can be detected at once as the other coins will be measurably colder.

The Coin in the Saucer

THE magician places a penny on a saucer and then pours a little water on top of it. He then asks the spectators if they can remove the penny without wet-

ting their fingers. It is an impossibility until the magician shows them how.

The *modus operandi* is a drinking glass containing some paper. The paper is ignited and, while it is burning, the glass is turned upside down and placed on the saucer. It should not cover the penny. The hot air in the glass will draw up all the water and the penny **can** be removed with dry fingers.

The Coin in the Sleeve

IN this trick, the performer tells his audience that he is going to do, openly, what magicians are so often accused of doing in secret, namely, put something up his sleeve. Suiting his actions to the words, he drops a quarter into his sleeve. Bringing his hand down, he shakes his arm as though to shake out the coin, but it has disappeared completely!

The quarter is not dropped into the sleeve at all, but into the performer's left breast coat pocket. The left forearm is held upright so the hand is almost level with the face. In this position, it covers the pocket and the sleeve opening is on a level with the pocket. The quarter is held between the right thumb and forefinger. Just before it is dropped into the pocket, the other fingers of the right hand are inserted in the sleeve ostensibly to open it up. Actually, this movement covers what really takes place.

Catching a Coin out of the Air

THIS is an excellent method to use to catch a coin out of the air. It can be employed by itself, or to produce a coin which is to be used in a following trick.

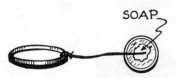

SOAP

The coin which is to be produced is attached, by means of a dab of soap, to the end of a short piece of thread which, in turn, is tied to a finger ring. The performer places the ring on his second finger, and the coin is then concealed behind his hand. To make the coin appear, the performer waves his hand in the air, and when ready, bends in his second finger. This brings the coin to the fingertips. They immediately catch hold of it. The coin can, of course, easily be detached from the thread.

The Rolling Coin Box

THIS is a variation of the famous stage trick known as the "Sliding Die Box" with which Thurston, among other great magicians, delighted his audiences at every performance. As done by Thurston, a large wooden die was placed in an oblong box which was just high enough to accommodate the die, but twice as long. In the front of the box were two doors. Thurston would close both doors and slide the die back and forth. Every one in the audience could plainly hear its movements. Then, holding the box at an angle, so the die was obviously at the lower end, Thurston would open the door at the opposite, or upper end.

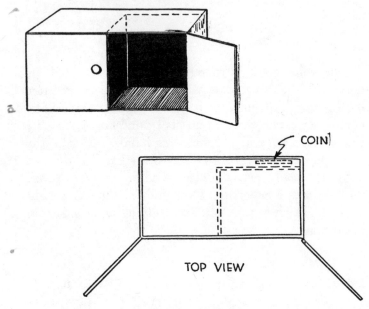

COIN

TOP VIEW

"See," he would say, "the die has disappeared."

Immediately people in the audience would shout, "Open the other door."

Thurston would tip the box the other way, and everybody would hear the die slide to the opposite end. Then he would open the door that had previously been closed. Finally, however, he opened both doors at the same time, and the box was revealed to be empty.

In the present version of the trick, a half-dollar is used instead of a die. The box is made out of an ordinary cardboard candy box fitted with two cardboard doors. The inside is painted dead black. Then a second smaller box is glued inside it, in the position shown in the drawing. Its interior is also painted dead black.

When doing the trick the performer places the half-dollar in the box and shuts both doors. Then he tilts the box, first one way and then the other. Every one hears the coin rolling to and fro. The doors are then opened alternately, as described above. The uppermost door is always the one to be opened, so the audience will believe the coin is in the opposite, or lower, end of the box.

When ready for the dénouement, the performer lets the coin roll into the little alleyway behind the inner box and opens both doors simultaneously. The box is seen to be empty. By pressing against the back of the box directly over the coin, the latter is held firmly in place and will not rattle as the box is tilted and even shaken to prove that the coin has really disappeared.

The Coin, Cards, and Glass Trick

THIS is an excellent and little-known trick which can be used to very good effect in conjunction with the "handkerchief coin vanish" previously described. The effect of the trick is as follows. The performer places a tumbler on his table and on top of it places a pack of cards. A coin is then wrapped up in a handkerchief, and the handkerchief is placed upon the cards. Presto! The audience hears a tinkling sound. The handkerchief is removed and opened out, and the coin is found to have vanished. The cards are lifted from the glass and within the glass is discovered the missing coin.

The secret lies in the preparation of the pack of cards. A group of specially prepared cards is used. Ten cards are prepared by cutting circular holes through their centers as shown in the first drawing. Three other cards are prepared by cutting slots in them shaped as shown in the second drawing. One of the first type of cards is placed face downwards on a table and the three slotted cards are glued on top of it. The nine remaining cards with holes through their centers are then glued in place above the slotted cards. This forms a little box, inside of which can be placed a coin. A hair-pin is then inserted in the slot to keep the coin from falling out. To the end of the hair-pin is attached a length of black thread.

The prepared cards and the coin hidden inside them are placed on the bottom of an ordinary pack on the magician's table. The tumbler is exhibited and the cards are then placed on top of it. The black thread should be on the end of the cards that faces the performer.

The next step is to pretend to wrap up a coin in a handkerchief. Actually, the performer retains the coin in his hand and wraps up, instead, a coin sewed into the corner of the handkerchief. The handkerchief is then placed on top of the cards, and as the performer

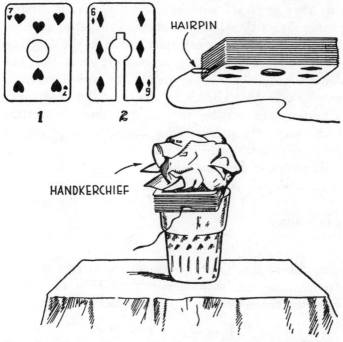

removes his hand, he grasps the black thread. When all is ready, he pulls gently on the thread. This pulls out the hair-pin and releases the duplicate coin which falls into the glass. The handkerchief is then picked up and shaken out, revealing the disappearance of the original coin. The cards are removed, and the glass with the coin inside it is passed to the audience for examination.

Pennies and Dimes

FOUR pennies and four dimes are placed in a row so that they alternate with one another, that is, first a penny, then a dime, then another penny, then another dime, and so on. The performer then asks the audience if they can bring all the pennies together and all the dimes together by moving them as follows. Two coins side by side must always be moved at the same time. This movement may be repeated three times only. After four moves, the pennies must all be together and so must the dimes.

The trick is done as follows:

1. Move the second and third coins from the left to the right end of the line. This places the coins in this position:

P x x D *P* D P D D P

2. Move the third and fourth coins from the left (those indicated by italicized letters) to the places indicated above by crosses. This places the coins thus:

P P D D x x P *D* *D* P

3. Move the sixth and seventh coins from the left (those indicated by italics) to the places indicated above by crosses. This places the coins thus:

P P D D D D P x x P

4. Move the two pennies at the left of the line to the places indicated by crosses. This brings the trick to a successful conclusion.

The Glass of Water Coin Vanish

THIS is a favorite method, with many professional magicians, of vanishing a coin. The coin that is to be made to disappear is covered with a handkerchief and held over a glass partially filled with water. The performer then releases the coin and it falls into the glass. Every one hears it tinkle as it strikes the sides of the glass, but when the handkerchief is lifted, the coin has disappeared.

The vanish is accomplished with the aid of a fake, which consists of a small round wrist-watch crystal. These can be obtained approximately the size of a half-dollar, and when using the fake, a half-dollar is always employed.

The performer pretends to cover the real half-dollar with the handkerchief, but instead of doing so, retains the half-dollar in his hand and substitutes the watch crystal, which he had previously secreted in the palm of his hand. The glass used when carrying out this vanish should be a small one, the bottom of which is the same size as the watch crystal.

Tricks with Matches and Match Boxes

The Penetrating Matches

A BOX of matches is opened and shown to be full and is then placed on one end on a table. The drawer is facing the audience so they can see the matches all the time. Suddenly the magician closes the drawer with a sharp blow. Reaching under the table, the magician produces a handful of matches. They are the ones that were in the box, for when it is opened it is empty.

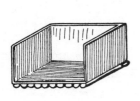
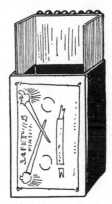

The box is empty right from the beginning of the trick, but it is made to appear full by a clever fake. This consists of a portion of a match-box drawer— about one third as long as the entire drawer. It is cut from a match box and to its bottom is glued a row of matches.

77

In doing the trick, the fake is placed in one end of an empty match box, the box being closed. The edges of the fake drawer are pushed in between the sides of the box and its regular drawer. The match side of the fake is turned towards the audience.

When the magician apparently strikes the drawer and drives it shut, he really grips the fake in his hand and removes it, placing it in his pocket at the first opportunity. With his other hand, he reaches under the table and produces some loose matches which had previously been placed on a chair pushed close in to the table. These are thrown on the table and the empty match box is then passed for examination.

Match Mind-reading

THIS is an exceptionally puzzling experiment. A match box is emptied onto the table and a spectator is asked to take as many as he likes. Let us assume that he takes 12. The performer then picks up some matches, counts them, and tells the spectator, "I have as many matches as you have, enough more to make 17, and 6 over." He asks the spectator how many matches he has and the answer is "Twelve." The performer counts out 12 matches, then 5 more to make 17, and then counts those left over. There are just 6!

The performer notes about how many matches the spectator picks up and makes sure to take a considerably greater number himself. Using the above example, we will assume that the spectator takes 12 matches, and when the performer counts those which he picks up, he finds they total 23. What he tells the spectator is simply another way of expressing the number 23. He does not know the exact number of matches held by the spectator, but can see that he has less than, say, 17. Accordingly, he says, "I have as many matches as you, and enough more to make 17. How many matches have you?" "Twelve." "Ah, I thought so," says the performer and counts out 12 matches. Then he says, "Enough more to make 17," and counts out 5 more matches. Since 17 from 23 leaves 6, he now has 6 matches left in his hand. He counts these out, and says, "And 6 left over." The effect is startling, though based on the simplest of mathematical calculations.

The Reducing Match Box

A SAFETY-MATCH box full of matches is shown the audience and then, with a pass of the magician's hand, it is reduced to one-half size.

The trick depends upon sleight of hand for its execution, but it is quite easy to do and a little practice will make any one proficient at it.

A small match box, one half as large as the ordinary penny box, is required and can be purchased at any large tobacco store. A few matches are removed from this small box, so that when the box is shaken the matches can be heard rattling inside it. The large box is filled completely so the matches will not rattle.

Before doing the trick, the drawer of the large box is opened far enough to permit the small box to be pushed in behind it (the drawer) until it is out of sight inside the cover of the large box. The large box can

then be exhibited quite freely, and no one will suspect that the small box is concealed inside it.

The large box is held in the left hand, the partially opened drawer pointing to the right. The magician then shuts the drawer, thus pushing the small box out into the left hand.

Now, there are two ways to get rid of the large box. One is to cover it with the right hand and carry it away in that hand. As this is done, the left hand is kept closed and is elevated. At the same time the performer shakes his left hand so the matches in the small box will rattle and keep the audience's attention on the left rather than the right hand. The magician then turns his left side towards the audience and drops the large match box into his right-hand coat pocket.

The other method of disposing of the large match

box is to have it attached throughout the trick to a piece of elastic cord which runs underneath the left-hand side of the coat to the belt loops of the trousers. In using this method, the large box is covered for an instant with both hands just after the drawer has been closed. During this instant, it is released and flashed out of sight beneath the coat. The magician then has his right hand free with which to make a few mystic passes over his left hand before opening it and revealing the reduction in the match box's size.

Passing Two Matches through Each Other

THE magician takes two matches, one in each hand, where he holds them between the thumb and forefinger. With a sudden movement he brings his hands together.

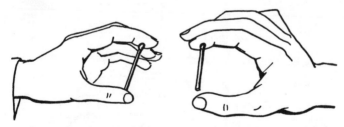

To all appearances, the matches pass right through each other, for they become linked together.

The trick must be done with non-safety-matches, for the tips of these matches become slightly sticky when they are dampened. Just before doing the trick, the magician wets the tip of his right forefinger. When the head of the right-hand match contacts the finger, it will stick to it tightly, after a moment's pressure has been applied.

Just as the hands approach each other, the performer lifts his right forefinger. This carries the match out of the way long enough for the left-hand match to pass by. The right forefinger is then brought back to its original position, so the match is held between it and the thumb.

The Balanced Match

THE magician gives matches to several of the spectators and asks if they can balance them on their thumbs. All try, but none can succeed, so the magician shows

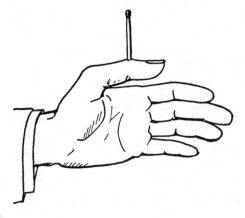

them that it can be done by balancing a match in an upright position on his own thumb.

The trick is done by placing the bottom of the match on the joint of the thumb, with the thumb bent slightly inwards. When the thumb is straightened out, the match will be tightly gripped in the small crease which crosses the knuckle and will stand quite firmly in an upright position.

The Penetrating Mark

THE magician lights a match and after it has burned for a moment blows it out. With the burned end he marks a line on the palm of his hand. Turning his hand over, he draws another line on the back. He then explains that by a certain kind of rubbing, he is able to force the mark on the back of his hand right through to the palm. He rubs out the line on the back of his hand, opens his palm, and the rubbed-out line is found there crossing the line originally drown on the palm.

The secret lies in the way the first line is drawn. It should be drawn diagonally across the palm from the forefinger towards the opposite side of the hand and should cross one of the lines of the hand. When the hand is closed, this line will make a duplicate of itself at right angles, thus forming a cross.

The Pencil from the Match Box

THE magician takes a match box from his pocket and opens the drawer. Peering inside, he shows signs of surprise and these are soon justified for he pulls a full-length pencil out of the box.

Before doing the trick, the pencil is hidden up the

left coat sleeve. The point should be just in the palm of the hand, and the back of the hand is kept turned towards the audience.

The match box has been prepared by cutting out one end of the drawer. This open end faces inwards towards the left wrist during the trick. When the box is opened, the pencil is inserted through the open end of the drawer, the fingers of the right hand grasp it and pull it through the box into view of the audience.

If one of the very long pencils, which are sold at some stores, can be obtained, it can be used to very good effect in this same deception.

The Color-changing Match Tips

THE magician shows his audience a match with a blue tip, one of the non-safety variety that comes in a large box. Placing it on a handkerchief, he folds the corners over. Upon unfolding the handkerchief, the tip of the match is found to be red.

The blue tip which is first shown to the audience is one which has previously been cut from another match and fastened to the lower end of a red-tipped match with a drop of glue. The match is held so its real tip, the red one, is hidden behind the fingers.

The match is placed on the handkerchief and covered with one of the corners. The performer then picks the match up near the false blue tip, keeping it covered by the handkerchief, under the folds of which he removes the blue tip entirely, leaving the match in its original red-tipped condition.

Matches from Nowhere

THIS is a very brilliant bit of impromptu magic which can be shown anywhere on the spur of the moment and well deserves a little practice in order to be sure of obtaining the full effect.

A clip of paper matches is exhibited and all the matches are torn out, the magician putting them in one of his pockets. The clip is then closed; the magician blows upon it, and opens it and it is once again full of matches.

Upon examining a clip of paper matches you will find that there are four irregularly spaced rows of matches. Before showing the trick, pull the front two rows slightly forward, so there will be a small space between them and the two rear rows.

When you open the clip, fold back the cover and tuck it between the two double rows of matches, thus concealing the rear rows. The two front rows are then torn out and disposed of and the cover is folded back into its original place on the front of the clip. When it is folded back again, the clip appears to be a new one entirely filled with matches.

The Transferred Colors

THE magician shows the audience a red and a blue piece of tissue-paper. He puts the red piece into an empty match box and marks a red cross on the end of the drawer. The blue piece is put into another match box which is marked with a blue cross. Waving his hands over the two boxes, the magician commands the papers to "Pass." The boxes are opened and the two pieces of paper are found to have changed places!

The preparation for this trick consists in marking a red cross on one end of the drawer of one of the match

boxes and a blue cross on one end of the other box prior
to the performance. This done, the drawers are pushed
partway open so the secret mark will be out of sight
beneath the box covers.

The red paper is put in the box previously marked
with a blue cross; and the blue paper is put in the box

RED PAPER   BLUE PAPER

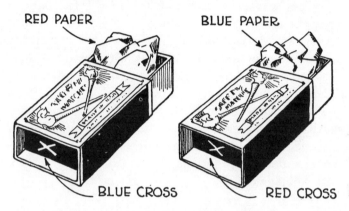

BLUE CROSS   RED CROSS

with a red cross. The opposite ends of the drawers are
colored to correspond to the paper put inside each box.

After the boxes have been shut, the magician turns to
go to his table and as he does so turns the boxes around
so the secret marks will face the audience when the
boxes are laid on the table. The rest of the trick then
takes care of itself.

The Obedient Matches

OPENING a box of safety-matches, the performer shows that it is full. The box is then turned upside down and, still in this position, the drawer is slowly removed. To every one's surprise, the matches do not fall out but resist the law of gravity even after the drawer is fully withdrawn. After holding the drawer for a moment, the magician motions downwards with his disengaged hand, and at this magic gesture, the spell is broken and the matches tumble out onto the table.

The matches are held in place by a broken match which is wedged tightly across the drawer on top of the other matches. The broken match is dislodged at the proper moment by squeezing the ends, which causes the sides to bulge out.

Match-box Eiffel Tower

A VERY respectable match-box Eiffel Tower can be made by balancing five or six match boxes, end to end, on top of each other. It looks like a feat requiring a considerable amount of real juggling ability, and by making the balancing appear precarious, the performer can make it appear much more difficult than it really is.

Actually, the match boxes are held quite firmly in place by pushing each one's drawer a short distance inside the box next below it. When fastened together by this means, they can even be tilted at an angle, and thus become a Leaning Tower of Pisa, without falling apart.

The Bewitched Matches

TAKING a box of matches from his pocket, the performer opens first one end, showing the audience the heads, and then opens the other end showing them the bottom of the matches.

Asking the audience to remember at which end the heads are, the magician immediately pushes open the

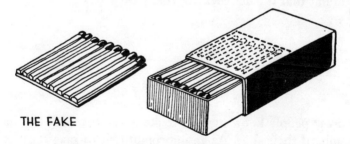

THE FAKE

end containing the bottoms of the matches. They have turned end for end, for the heads of the matches appear. He opens the other end of the box and the heads are there again. The box is closed; the same end is pushed open and the bottom ends are where the heads were an instant before.

The trick is done by means of a cleverly made fake. It is made by cutting a row of matches in half and gluing the head ends to a piece of the thin wood taken from the bottom of a match box. This fake is placed in a partially filled box of matches, with the heads facing in the opposite direction to the heads of the real matches.

When starting the trick the fake heads should be covering the bottoms of the real matches. The box is opened and the real heads are shown. Then, by slanting the box and giving it an imperceptible shake, the fake slides down to the opposite end and the bottoms of the real bottom ends are shown.

Thereafter, by sliding the fake to and fro, the magician can make heads or bottoms appear at either end he chooses, until the audience is bewildered and ready to admit that the matches are really betwitched.

A Striking Effect

FEW people know how to strike a safety-match on the sole of their shoe. As an impromptu bit of magic, or as an effect sandwiched in between two other match tricks, it is always a puzzle to the audience.

It is done by rubbing the side of a safety-match box against the sole of the shoe near the heel, where it will not come in contact with the floor and rub off. This, in effect, makes a match box out of your shoe and you will

have no difficulty in striking several matches on it before the substance wears off.

The Magnetic Match-box Drawer

PLACE the drawer of a safety-match box upside down
on the table and on top of it place the cover, standing
it upright on one end. Then ask the audience if they
can lift the cover and the drawer at the same time,
without, however, touching the drawer.

It is impossible to do this in any way but one. That
is by taking the upper end of the cover between your
lips and drawing in your breath, at the same time raising your head. The suction will cause the drawer to
stick fast to the cover and both of them will be lifted
together.

Tricks with Balls

Ball from the Air

THIS is a very effective method of snatching a ball out of the air, after showing the hand to be empty. The ball appears at the fingertips when the magician reaches out into the air for it, no handkerchief or other covering being used.

The ball is one of the small rubber ones usually sold

with an elastic attached so it can be bounced. The elastic is removed and in its place is put a piece of thread about an inch long. The other end of the thread is fastened to a finger ring which the magician wears on the second finger of his right hand.

The ball hangs down in back of the hand, and, with fingers pointing upwards, the palm of the hand can be shown to be empty. To make the ball appear, the hand should be extended quite rapidly and at the same time turned forward. This will swing the ball instantaneously to the tips of the fingers. The left hand can then take it and, by a sharp pull, break the thread.

The Disappearing Ball

A BALL of the same type as that described in the last trick is used for the present effect in which a ball held at the magician's fingertips, is tossed into the air and disappears.

The ball is fastened to a length of elastic cord which is passed through the belt loops on the performer's trousers and knotted to the loop on the left side. The cord should be of such a length that when the ball is held in the right hand, it will be stretched tight enough to pull the ball instantaneously back under the coat.

Before doing the trick, the ball is placed in the lower right-hand vest pocket. From there, it is taken in the right hand and shown to the audience. Then, with his right side towards the audience, the magician makes a motion as if to toss the ball into the air. As he does so, he lets go of the ball and it flies out of sight beneath his coat.

Mysterious Ball Tube

THE magician shows the audience a cardboard tube about a foot long and two inches in diameter. A ball is dropped through it to show that it is unprepared in any way. Once again, the ball is dropped into the tube,

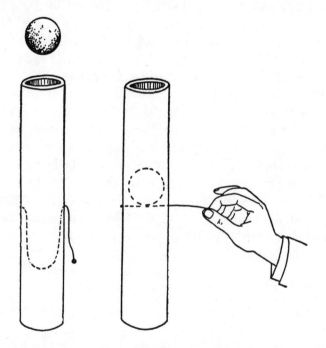

but this time it does not come out the bottom. Some mysterious form of magnetism has held it in the tube. The magician is careful to show that he is not holding the ball by the pressure of his fingers. At his word of command, the spell is broken and the ball continues its descent through the tube, falling out the bottom into the magician's hand.

The mechanism which stops the ball's descent is the magician's old friend—a piece of black thread. The tube itself is an ordinary mailing tube which is easy to procure. A knot is tied in one end of the thread, and the other end is passed through two holes drilled opposite to each other about midway of the tube's length. An end about an inch and a half long is left outside the tube and a small bead is tied to the extreme end. If the tube is painted black, the thread will not be detectable.

As long as the thread is allowed to hang loose, the ball will pass freely through the tube. By drawing the thread tight and thus stretching it across the tube, the ball will be stopped. The best way to manipulate the thread is by using the right thumb—the tube being held in the right hand. The bead is on the side of the tube towards the performer, as is also the thumb. By sliding the thumb downwards along the tube, thus pushing the bead downward, the thread will be drawn taut and will stop the ball.

The Ball in the Glass

THE magician shows the audience a small rubber ball which he places in a drinking glass and covers with a handkerchief. A few magic words are uttered, and when

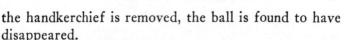

the handkerchief is removed, the ball is found to have disappeared.

This vanish is accomplished by means of the ingenious arrangement shown in the accompanying illustration. The ball is fastened to the middle of one side of the handkerchief by a length of black thread. This is in-

visible to the audience. When presenting the trick, the performer holds the ball in his left hand and the hand-kerchief in his right hand. Both hands are kept quite close together, so the thread will not be broken. The ball is dropped into the glass and covered with the handkerchief, the handkerchief being placed so the side to which the thread is attached is nearest to the per-former. When the handkerchief is removed, it is lifted by the two corners nearest to the performer and the ball is consequently hidden behind it where the audience can-not see it.

The Balanced Ball

THE magician passes two balls for examination. They may be golf balls or rubber balls. Receiving them back, he places one on top of the other and waves his hands above and around them to mesmerize them. The top ball balances on the lower one. In this trick, it is quite effective to have two balls of different sizes, first to balance the larger one on the smaller one and then place the smaller one on top of the larger one.

The secret of the balance is a little dab of soap or wax which the magician presses onto one of the balls when he gets them back from the audience. When putting the balls together, this adhesive substance comes at the point of contact between them and holds them together.

The Ball Beneath the Handkerchief

THE effect of this trick is almost too good to be true. It should be practised carefully and shown judiciously, for it is a real mystery. What happens is that the magician shows the audience a small rubber ball which he holds in his right hand. He throws a handkerchief over his hand and then asks the members of the audience to reach under the handkerchief and make sure that the ball is still there. Each person feels the ball, but as soon as the last person has felt it, the magician pulls off the handkerchief and the ball has vanished.

The hand is covered once more, and the audience is asked to reach under the handkerchief to satisfy themselves that the ball is not there. After all are agreed that the magician's hand is empty, he removes the handkerchief and "Presto," there is the ball.

Obviously, no strings or elastics are used to make the ball vanish and reappear, but, what no one suspects, the magician has a confederate. He is the person who is last to reach under the handkerchief to see if the ball is still there. When he does so, he takes the ball in his own hand and removes it.

It is by the same method that the ball is made to reappear. The confederate is the last person to reach under the handkerchief to make sure that the magician's hand is still empty. Under cover of the handkerchief, he drops the ball into the performer's hand and a moment later, the handkerchief is removed and the returned ball is revealed.

Mysterious Rolling Ball

THIS is a very novel and little-known trick which practically defies detection. A ball, either a golf ball or a small rubber ball, is passed for examination and upon being returned is placed on the magician's table. The magician waves his hands over it and it starts to roll along the table to the left. After it has nearly reached the edge of the table, the magician gestures towards the right with his hands and the ball reverses its direction and goes to the right. During the course of the trick, the magician several times stands away from the ball and removes his hands from its vicinity to show that no

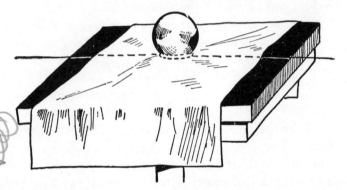

threads run between his hands and the ball. The ball can also be picked up and tossed in the air, or to the audience for examination, to show that it is unprepared in any way.

The secret of the ball's motion is a small ring, with two long black threads attached to it. The ring is underneath the cloth covering the table and the threads run off to left and right to assistants. An ideal place to use as a stage for this trick, and for many others where bits of apparatus, prepared cards, or assistants are needed, is the doorway between two rooms. This forms a natural proscenium and there is always ample room for assistants and tables to hold the different objects to be used during the performance.

Tricks with Handkerchiefs

The End

Appearing and Disappearing Handkerchief

THE simply made piece of apparatus described herewith will prove most useful for vanishing silk handkerchiefs and causing them to reappear again. It is used by
all professional magicians.

It consists of a small, hollow rubber ball in one side
of which is cut a circular hole with a diameter of seven-

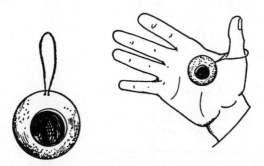

eighths of an inch (see illustration). Two small holes
are then made near the hole and a piece of fine, flesh-
colored silk thread is fastened through them so as to
form a loop. This loop should be just big enough so
that when it is placed around the thumb the ball will
rest in the hollow of the palm.

When about to vanish a handkerchief, the ball is concealed in the right hand, the loop being over the thumb.
The performer stands with his left side towards the

audience. The handkerchief is taken between the two hands, which are moved slowly up and down, while the fingers gradually tuck the handkerchief into the ball. When the handkerchief is well inside, the ball is rolled over to the back of the right hand. The hands are then separated and the palms are shown to be empty. With a little practice, the hands can be reversed and the backs shown. The right hand is simply turned over and the ball is allowed to slip into the palm during the slow turning movement.

The handkerchief can, of course, be made to reappear by reversing the process described above.

The Handkerchief "Pull"

EVERY magician should make himself what is known as a handkerchief "pull," which is the favorite professional device used for vanishing a handkerchief. "Pulls" of different types can be purchased at any magic store, but the one described herewith is easy and inexpensive to make and is perfectly adequate.

Get a hollow rubber ball of the type generally sold with an elastic attached for a nickel. With a sharp knife cut a circular hole about three-quarters of an inch in diameter in one side. Opposite this hole, make a small puncture. Thread a piece of elastic cord through this small hole, fastening it by means of a large knot tied on the inside.

When using the "pull" the free end of the cord should be fastened to the belt strap on the left side of the trousers. From there it is run through the other belt straps, and should be of such a length that the "pull" rests on the right hip. Immediately before using it, how-

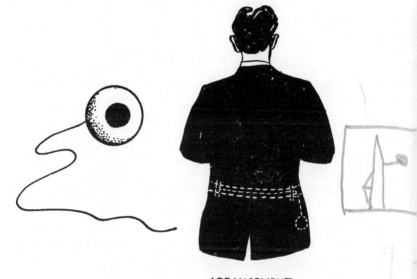

ARRANGEMENT
BENEATH COAT

ever, the "pull" should be placed in the right-hand vest pocket.

The handkerchief to be vanished is held in the left hand, and the "pull" is removed secretly from the vest pocket and held in the right hand. The performer's right side is turned towards the audience. Both hands are brought together and moved up and down, while the fingers tuck the handkerchief into the "pull." When it is well inside, the "pull" is released and flies out of sight beneath the coat.

Tying a Handkerchief with One Hand

THIS is a very surprising magical flourish which, if practised until it can be done rapidly, will be exceptionally mystifying. In effect, a handkerchief is placed in the right hand. The magician waves his hand, Presto! a knot appears in the center of the handkerchief.

The handkerchief is twisted diagonally and is then laid across the palm of the right hand, stretching from the fingers to the wrist. About one half the handkerchief should hang down below the wrist.

To tie the knot, the hand is bent forward and the fingers and thumb grasp the end that hangs down below the wrist. This end is then pulled upward, across the part that stretches over the hand, and through the loop that has been formed by the foregoing movements. The handkerchief is then given a quick shake and the knot will be found in its center.

The Dissolving Knot

THERE are several methods of tying two corners of a handkerchief together, or else knotting two handkerchiefs, and subsequently having the knot dissolve away

when blown upon by the magician. This is one of the best.

The secret is as follows. Before tying the knot, the performer crosses the corners of the handkerchief in the manner shown in the illustration. He then ties the corners into a single knot. Now, no matter how tightly the knot is drawn, a shake of the handkerchief will cause it to disappear.

The Mystic Knot

THE magician ties a single knot in the center of a hand-kerchief and pulls on the corners until the knot is drawn quite tight. He then undoes the knot and tells the spectators that he proposes to tie a single knot in the hand-kerchief, as before, and to untie it by pulling on the

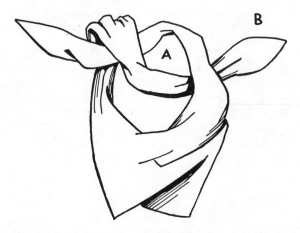

same two corners. This, naturally, appears to be impossible, but the magician, as usual, succeeds in carrying out his promise.

The trick is done as follows. When the knot has been tied, the performer opens it up and passes his left hand through its center, A, as shown in the drawing. He grasps the right hand corner, B, between his left thumb and forefinger, and takes the other or left hand corner, between his right thumb and forefinger. He then draws

his left hand back through the center of the knot. This unties the knot, exactly according to the conditions laid down at the beginning of the trick.

The Drinking-glass Handkerchief Vanish

THIS is a most startling method of vanishing a handkerchief which has been used, because of its brilliant effect, by a number of professional magicians. A colored silk handkerchief is used, such as can be obtained at any ten-cent store. It is placed in a drinking glass which is held, horizontally, between the open palms of the performer's hands. Holding the glass and handkerchief in full view, the performer exclaims "Pass!" and the handkerchief instantly vanishes. The glass is then passed for examination to show that it does not contain a mirror or any other apparatus.

The handkerchief which is used is prepared by sewing to its center a length of thin, but strong, cord. The free end of the cord is passed up the performer's right arm beneath the coat sleeve and is tied around the left wrist. The cord should be of such a length that when the arms hang down naturally, the handkerchief will rest in the right hand; but that when the arms are outstretched, the handkerchief will be pulled up beneath the right coat sleeve.

In doing the trick, the glass is held in the left hand and the handkerchief is placed inside it. The right hand

is then placed on top of the glass which is turned to a horizontal position. The glass is moved slowly up and down a few times and then, with the left fingers clutching the bottom of the glass tightly, the arms are suddenly stretched out, the right hand momentarily letting go of the glass. The handkerchief flashes up the right sleeve and the right hand is instantly replaced.

The Handkerchief Pyramid

TAKING a handkerchief from his pocket, the performer unfolds it and places it spread out upon the table. Grasping it by the center, he raises his hand until the handkerchief is in the shape of a pyramid and is almost lifted off the table.

Waving his other hand, as though to mesmerize the handkerchief, the magician lets go with the hand holding the handkerchief's center. Instead of falling in a crumpled heap, the handkerchief defies the laws of gravity and remains upright. To prove that it is not supported by a thread, the magician passes his hands above and around it and finally picks it up and passes it to the audience for inspection.

The secret lies in the use of a newly laundered handkerchief which has been slightly starched and ironed. When in this condition, its natural stiffness and the slight added support afforded by the creases are sufficient to keep it standing in its pyramidal position.

The Flying Handkerchief

THIS trick requires a little practice until the knack of doing it is acquired, but it is well worth the time spent in mastering it.

In effect, the performer holds a handkerchief by two of its diagonally opposite corners, one in his left hand and one in his right. At the word of command, the handkerchief suddenly seems to come to life and darts away towards one side. The magician no sooner catches it than it flies to the opposite side, and it will continue springing back and forth, traveling several feet each time, until the magician commands it to stop.

It is quite easy to convince an audience that this effect is obtained by cleverly concealed rubber bands, but actually no apparatus is needed. Suppose you wish to make the handkerchief fly to the left. Simply draw the right hand corner out as far as you can and then let go with the right hand, immediately afterwards letting go with the left hand. As the handkerchief darts away, the left hand follows it and catches it before it is out of reach.

The Hat and Handkerchief Trick

THIS trick is done with the magician seated behind a table. It is a very good dinner-table trick as it can be done appropriately at the table and is difficult to detect even when under close observation.

A coin is laid on the table and the magician covers it with a soft felt hat. After a moment, the hat is lifted but the coin is still there. The hat is replaced and in a moment or two, the magician lifts it just a little way and looks anxiously beneath it. The coin is still in its place, but the magician, nothing daunted, replaces the hat and commands "Pass." At once, he lifts the hat and there beneath it is a handkerchief, apparently large enough to fill the entire hat.

The handkerchief is rolled up into as small a ball as possible before doing the trick and is placed in the performer's lap. The first time the hat is lifted, it is picked up by the left hand which moves it over to the edge of the table. While the magician is looking at the coin and thus directing the audience's attention to it, the right hand pushes the handkerchief up into the hat. The left hand grasps it through the felt.

The hat is then replaced, the left hand maintaining its grip. In a moment, the left hand raises the hat a little ways and the magician peeks under it, drawing attention to the fact that the coin is there, but nothing else.

As soon as the hat is again placed over the coin, the left hand is removed. This frees the handkerchief, and a moment afterwards the hat is lifted for the final time and the handkerchief is revealed.

The Fireproof Handkerchief

THIS is a most startling effect which appears to be against the laws of nature. The magician passes a handkerchief to and fro through the flame of a candle and it does not catch fire.

The handkerchief is prepared by soaking it in a solution of borax and water. This makes it very nearly fireproof and it can be passed back and forth through the flame as often as desired without catching fire.

The Dissolving Knot

THIS is a very baffling deception. The performer goes through the motions of tying a knot in a handkerchief, and to the audience, there appeared to be a knot but when he pulls on the ends of the handkerchief to tighten it, the knot mysteriously disappears.

The "knot" is tied as follows. The handkerchief is held by opposite corners stretched in front of the performer. The right hand moves forward and then to the left, describing a semicircle around the left hand. It is brought to rest when it is on the left-hand side of, and above, the left wrist. It is then brought to the right, passing over the left hand, and the corner of the handkerchief it holds is passed through the loop that has been formed *from the outer side,* or the side away from the performer's body. The hands are then pulled apart, and the "knot" dissolves away.

The Handkerchief and the Four Boxes

FOUR small rectangular cardboard boxes are exhibited. Each has marked on its cover a large number—1, 2, 3, and 4. The magician borrows a lady's handkerchief and places it in Box No. 1, and then asks the audience to select one of the other boxes. Presto! The handkerchief vanishes from Box No. 1 and reappears in the box chosen by the spectators.

The method of preparing the boxes is as follows. On the cover of each one is drawn a large figure 1. Three pieces of cardboard are then cut out, each the same in size as the covers of the boxes. On both sides of one piece is drawn a large figure 2, on both sides of the next a figure 3, and on both sides of the third a figure 4. These pieces are then fastened, with a single dab of wax or soap to the tops of three of the boxes. The fourth box is not provided with a false cover; but four dabs of wax or soap are stuck to its top, one at each corner.

The borrowed handkerchief is placed in the last mentioned box on the cover of which appears the number 1, and the performer holds this box in his left hand. The audience then selects one of the other boxes, say, No. 3. The performer picks it up and then, apparently wishing to push the other two boxes to one side, places No. 3 box, *upside down,* on the No. 1 box in his left hand. He then clears a space on the table with his right hand, and while he is doing so, turns over the boxes in his left hand. This places the No. 1 box, containing the handkerchief, on top. The audience believe, however, that

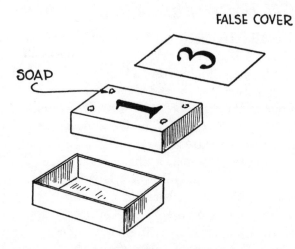

FALSE COVER

SOAP

the No. 3 box, which is empty, is on top. As the boxes used are small ones easily held in the palm of the hand, this turning-over movement is simple to execute unobserved.

The performer now turns his attention to the two boxes in his left hand. He lifts up the uppermost one, but as he does so, he presses down on it firmly so the false cover on the underneath box, bearing the figure 3, adheres to it. When the box is lifted, it is labeled 3, and the audience believes it to be the same No. 3 box just taken, empty, from the table. The underneath box, relieved of its false cover, is now labeled 1.

The trick has now been completed. All that remains is to open the No. 1 box and show it to be empty, then to open the No. 3 box and discover the borrowed handkerchief inside it.

The Handkerchief Vases

IN this trick the magician ties together two blue silk handkerchiefs and places them in a round glass vase. He then exhibits a red handkerchief and places it in another similar vase. A handkerchief is placed over the second vase and when it is removed the red handkerchief has vanished. The two blue handkerchiefs are then withdrawn from their vase and the red handkerchief is discovered tied between them.

The best type of "vase" to use for this trick is a cut-glass sugar bowl, such as can be purchased at the ten-cent store. Two of these are needed and each is fitted with a shiny metal fake, or mirror, as shown in the drawing on the next page. The fakes are cut out of tin; even a tin can will do, if no other tin is available. When they are in place, the vases will appear to be empty.

Before doing the trick the performer places two blue handkerchiefs with a red handkerchief tied between them behind the fake in one of the vases. These handkerchiefs are rolled up so that the red handkerchief cannot be seen.

When doing the trick the performer ties together two blue handkerchiefs and places them in the front half of the vase. In returning the glass to the table, he

turns it around, so the two blue handkerchiefs with the red one between them are toward the audience.

The single red handkerchief is then placed in the second vase. It is covered with a large handkerchief and as this is done, the performer turns the vase around. When the large handkerchief is removed, the vase appears to be empty. The handkerchiefs in the other vases are then removed, and the red handkerchief is discovered between the two blue ones.

The Handkerchief on the String

THE performer asks the audience to tie the ends of a piece of string about three feet long to his two wrists, so the string stretches between them. He then takes a handkerchief, two corners of which have been tied together, and turns his back for a moment. When he again faces the audience the handkerchief is on the middle of the string.

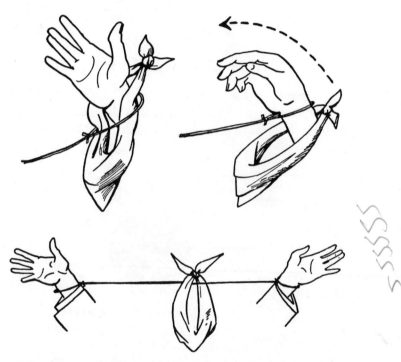

The trick is done as follows. Pass the handkerchief beneath the string that encircles the right wrist, and over the fingers of the right hand, as shown in the drawing. When this has been done, the handkerchief is around the right wrist. The left hand then takes hold of it at the point where the knot is shown in the drawing, and brings the knot around and over the right hand. The handkerchief will then be knotted around the length of string between the wrists.

The Color Changing Handkerchief

THIS is one of the most beautiful of all handkerchief sleights and is an effect that is used by almost all the professional magicians. In performing it, the magician

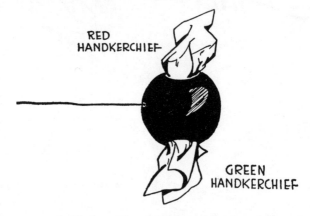

RED
HANDKERCHIEF

GREEN
HANDKERCHIEF

pushes a red silk handkerchief into his closed fist. As it passes through his fist, it changes color and emerges a bright green.

The trick is performed with a small piece of apparatus known as a "color-changing pull," such as is shown in the drawing. A home-made pull is made from a small, hollow rubber ball. Two holes are cut in it opposite one another, as shown, and a long piece of cord elastic is attached to it. The elastic is passed through a small hole and knotted on the inside.

Prior to the performance, the magician passes the elastic from left to right through the belt straps of his trousers and ties the loose end to the belt strap furthest to the right. The cord should be of such a length that, when this has been done, the pull will rest against his left hip. Here it is hidden by his coat. Inside the pull is stuffed a green silk handkerchief.

When doing the trick, the performer gets the pull into his left hand. He then takes a red handkerchief and with his right forefinger pushes it slowly down into his closed left hand. As it goes into his hand, it enters the uppermost hole in the pull and pushes the green handkerchief out. When the red silk is all inside the pull, the performer removes the green silk with his right hand and holds it aloft. As he does so, he releases the pull and the elastic flashes it back out of sight beneath his coat. The left hand is then shown empty.

Another Handkerchief Color Change

THIS is a more elaborate version of the color-changing handkerchief trick. In the present trick, three white handkerchiefs are pushed through a tube made, in front

of the audience, from a piece of paper. When the handkerchiefs emerge, they are three different colors, red,
blue, and yellow.

The trick is done with the aid of the fake which is
shown in the drawing. This is a piece of 1½ inch mailing tube about three inches long. Inside it is glued a
piece of tape as shown. Prior to showing the trick, the
three colored handkerchiefs are pushed into this fake.

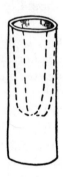

The fake keeps them from going all the way through.

The fake is placed on the magician's table and on top
of it are placed the three white handkerchiefs. Near-by
is a piece of white paper measuring about twelve inches
square.

When presenting the trick, the performer first picks
up the piece of paper and shows it, back and front, to
the audience. He then holds the paper in his right hand
and lowers it to the table to a point right beside the
white handkerchiefs. With his left hand he picks up the
white handkerchiefs and simultaneously moves the piece
of paper over to cover the fake.

After exhibiting the white handkerchiefs, the performer returns them to the table. He then picks up the square of paper, and with it picks up the fake, which is kept in back of the paper. The paper is then rolled up into a tube around the fake.

The tube is then held in the left hand and the white handkerchiefs are pushed into it one by one. As they enter the fake they force out the colored handkerchiefs which emerge slowly from the bottom of the tube. The performer pulls them out with his right hand, and as he removes the last one, he loosens his grasp on the tube and allows the fake to fall into his hand. He then places the last handkerchief and the fake on his table, and, with both hands free, unrolls the tube and shows the paper back and front.

Tricks with Rings

Vanishing a Ring Wrapped in Paper

THE performer borrows a wedding-ring, or else produces one of his own (purchased at the ten-cent store),
and proceeds to wrap it up in a piece of paper. The
paper is handed to a spectator who is requested to un-
wrap it. When he does so, it is discovered that the
ring has disappeared.

This excellent little method of vanishing a ring is
accomplished by means of a duplicate ring. The duplicate is tied to a length of cord elastic, and the free end
of the elastic is lead from left to right through the
trouser belt straps and tied to the strap furthest to
the right. The elastic should be of such a length that the
ring rests in front of the second belt strap from the
front. This strap is usually right over the left hand
trousers' pocket.

When presenting the trick, the duplicate ring is gotten into the left hand. The other, or borrowed ring, is
taken in the right hand, and the performer pretends to
transfer it to the left hand and produces the duplicate
ring at his left fingertips.

He then places the paper on his table and puts the
duplicate ring on it, retaining his grasp, however, so
it will not fly away. He folds over the side of the paper
furthest away from him. Then, as he folds over one
side of the paper, he releases the ring and it flies out

of sight beneath his coat. The folding is then com-
leted and the trick carried on to its dénouement.

Instantaneous Ring Release

THIS is a very rapid action, with a surprising effect.
One end of a looped string is passed through a ring and
the other end is then passed through the first loop. As

this is difficult to describe clearly, the way it is done is
shown in the accompanying diagram.

Two spectators are asked to grasp the string at the
points marked A and B, while the magician grasps the
loop at C. The spectators are told to pull the parts
they are holding clear of the ring, and to pull on them
steadily, the magician, meanwhile, pulling against them.

The magician then suddenly commands "Pass!" and
the ring drops free of the string.

This is accomplished by the magician simply releasing
the loop which he is holding. To the audience, however, it appears as though the ring had passed right
through the string.

The Disappearing Ring

THE magician borrows a ring from some member of the audience and wraps it up in a handkerchief. He offers the handkerchief to several spectators and asks them to feel the ring to make sure that it is there. This

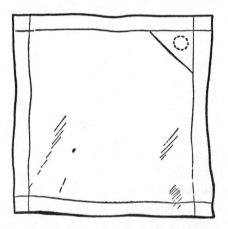

is done, but an instant later the performer shakes out the handkerchief and the ring has disappeared.

This is accomplished by means of a specially prepared handkerchief. It has a ten-cent store wedding-ring sewed in one corner which is covered with a piece of material identical with that of which the handkerchief is made. Thus, it is invisible from either side of the handkerchief.

The borrowed ring is taken in the left hand and the handkerchief is draped over it. The ring is secreted in the palm of the left hand. As this is done, the sewed-in ring is pushed up to the center of the handkerchief by the right hand which then releases it and grasps it through the folds of the handkerchief. The left hand carries away the borrowed ring. The handkerchief can then be unfolded at any time and the ring will have disappeared.

The Ring in the Lemon

IN this trick, a ring is vanished and caused to reappear in a lemon selected by the audience from several that are offered them on a plate. The effect is heightened to a considerable extent, however, by the fact that the magician runs a threaded needle through the lemon and the ring is discovered on the thread.

The secret lies in the use of several duplicate rings, say four or five, which are purchased at the ten-cent store. Before presenting the trick, a number of lemons equal to the number of rings which have been obtained are prepared by cutting slits in them and inserting the rings in the slits. The slits should be just small enough to permit the rings to enter and should be cut in the middle of each lemon. The rings are pushed in until they reach the center of the lemons, so that when the needle is run through from end to end it will be sure to pass through the center of the ring.

The ring may be vanished by wrapping it in a handkerchief as described in "The Disappearing Ring," or else by having it attached to a piece of elastic cord which runs beneath the coat and through the belt loops of the trousers.

When doing the trick, have the lemons produced at the beginning and after one has been selected, place it by itself on a plate. Slice it at several points but do not cut it quite through. Then run the needle and thread through the lemon from end to end.

The lemon and the duplicate ring are now all prepared for the dénouement, so it is in order to proceed with the vanishing of the original ring. When this has been done, the slices of the lemon are removed one by one, until the middle one containing the duplicate ring is arrived at.

The Ring-and-Egg Trick

A RING is borrowed from one of the spectators and wrapped in a handkerchief. Upon the handkerchief being unfolded, the ring has disappeared. The performer, however, offers the audience a dish full of eggs and asks them to select one. The chosen egg is placed in an egg cup; the performer breaks its shell with a button-hook, reaches inside, and withdraws the vanished ring on the hook.

The ring is made to disappear by means of the prepared handkerchief previously described.

After it has supposedly been wrapped up in the handkerchief, the dish of eggs is shown the audience and one is selected. While this is being done, the magician goes to his table to pick up the egg cup and the button-hook. The bottom of the egg cup has been covered with soap prior to the performance, and the borrowed ring

is stuck upright in the soap. When an egg has been selected, the performer takes it and puts it in the cup, pressing down hard enough so the ring breaks the shell.

The handkerchief is shaken out and the ring is found to have disappeared. The performer then breaks the top of the egg, inserts the button-hook, and engages it in the loop of the ring, which he withdraws and exhibits to the audience.

The Ring on the String

THIS is an excellent mystery, for it is worked so quickly that what is accomplished appears to be absolutely impossible. In effect, the ends of a piece of string about eighteen inches long are tied around the performer's wrists. He is then given a bracelet which has been examined to make sure that it is solid. The performer steps behind a screen, and reappears in an instant with the bracelet threaded on the string between his wrists.

The trick is done by the use of two identical bracelets. These can be purchased at any ten-cent store. Before presenting the trick, the performer slips one of these over one of his wrists and pushes it up his arm beneath the coat sleeve so it is well concealed. As soon as he steps behind the screen, he puts the other ring in one of his pockets and pulls the ring on his arm down over his hand and onto the string.

The beauty of this trick is the speed with which it can be executed and a little practice to insure smooth and rapid work will be well repaid, for the effect is truly startling.

The Climbing Ring

THE magician borrows a ring, slips it onto a pencil, and, at his word of command, the ring climbs up and down, stops when told to, and finally jumps right off the end of the pencil into the air.

Once again, the secret *modus operandi* is a piece of black thread. It should be about two feet long. One end is tied around a small pin which is pushed into the eraser on the end of a lead pencil. The other end is left to hang free.

In presenting the trick, the pencil is picked up in the left hand and the right hand slips the ring over it. As soon as the right hand has let go of the ring, it travels along the pencil and unobtrusively grasps the free end of the thread. The pencil is held vertically and by moving it away from the body and back again, the ring is made to climb up and down at will. The final jump is caused by a rapid outward movement of the pencil. During these movements, the right hand is held motionless close to the body.

At the conclusion of the trick, the magician can ask the audience to pick the ring up from the floor and while they are doing so, the pin can be withdrawn and dropped on the floor together with its attached thread. The pencil can then be passed for examination.

Tricks with String

The Disappearing Knot

MAKE a single knot in the center of a piece of string and then tie the two ends together, so the string is formed into a figure 8, with the single knot in the center. The problem is to untie the single knot without untying the two ends of the string. Although it appears impossible, the magician turns his back for a moment or asks one of the audience to throw a handkerchief over

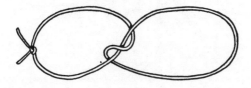

the string, and an instant later, produces the string from which the single knot has completely disappeared.

The trick is done very simply, but in spite of this, the effect is always very surprising. All you have to do to "untie" the knot is to slide it up to where the two ends of the string are tied together. Here it merges with the other knot and cannot be seen.

The Interwoven String

THIS is one of the best of the string tricks, for the string apparently passes right through all the fingers of one hand around which it has been interwoven.

The string, which is in the form of a loop, is threaded on the left hand in the following manner.

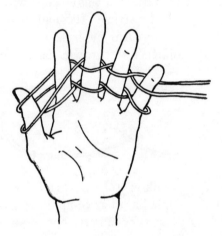

Holding the left hand palm up, place the loop over the left little finger. Cross the front string, or the one on the palm side of the hand, over the back string, and slip the two strings over the third finger. This leaves the strings crossed in between the two fingers. Repeat this process with the other two fingers, each time crossing the front string over the back string.

The strings are then passed around the thumb, care being taken that the string on the back side of the first finger is uppermost, or nearest to the top of the thumb.

In threading the string back over the fingers, place the string which was at the back of the first finger (and which was uppermost on the thumb), in back of the first finger again. Then cross the front string over the back string as before, looping the string over each finger. The method of interweaving is made clear by the diagrams.

To release the string, slip the left thumb free of its encircling loop, and pull on the opposite end of the string with your right hand. The string apparently passes right through all the fingers and comes completely free.

Passing a String through a Finger

TIE the two ends of a piece of string together and make a loop in one end. Care must be taken, when making the loop, to cross the right-hand string over the left-hand one, as shown in the drawing. Now place the loop between your teeth at the point A, put the right forefinger through the small loop at B, and pull the larger loop taut with the left hand.

Lower the right forefinger and bring it and the small loop out to the right of the large loop. Pass the tip of the finger over the right string of the large loop and under the left string, and then put the fingertip against your nose. Let go with your teeth and pull with your left hand. The string will apparently pass through your right forefinger.

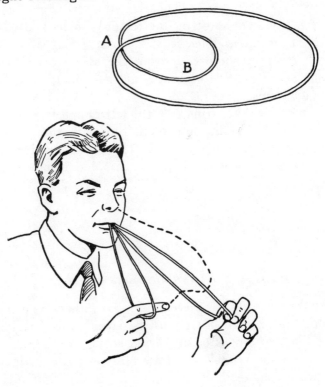

The Mysterious Knot

THE performer takes a long piece of string and asks some one in the audience to tie the ends around his wrist. This leaves a single length of string between his two hands. Turning his back for a moment, the magician then faces the audience again. By some mysterious means, a knot has been tied in the middle of the string.

The knot is tied as follows. The center of the string is grasped with both hands and made into a loop, this loop is then pushed up under the string encircling the left wrist. It is then given a twist and passed right over the left hand. Next push the loop under the string at the back of the left wrist and pull it over the fingers. This will complete the tying of the knot.

The String and Straw Trick (*1*)

THE magician threads a piece of string through a straw and then bends the middle of the straw to form an acute angle. Taking a pair of scissors, he cuts the straw in two, at the point where the angle is found. Although it is obvious that the string must have been cut through, the magician calmly pulls the two halves of the straw apart and there, inside, is the string in one piece with absolutely no sign of a scissor mark.

The secret lies in the use of a short piece of straw bent at an angle which the magician has hidden in his right hand prior to showing the trick.

After the real straw has been bent, the magician gets the short piece of straw between his right thumb and forefinger where it appears to be the center of the original straw. This is cut through with the scissors and the magician then twists the real straw to make it easier to

THE FAKE

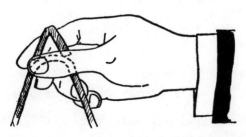

break, and pulls at each end. The straw will easily separate into two halves, which can be drawn apart revealing the string intact.

The String and Straw Trick (2)

THIS is another method of doing the string-and-straw trick, which is preferred by some magicians to the method previously described.

The straw is prepared by cutting a slit about two inches long in one of its sides. When the straw is bent this slit should be on the under side. The performer

pulls on the ends of the strings and this brings the
string down through the slit into the position shown in
the drawing. It is concealed from the audience by the

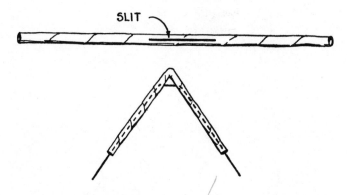

performer's hand holding the straw. The bent portion
of the straw is then cut off, but the scissors miss the
string entirely.

Tricks with Cigarettes and Cigars

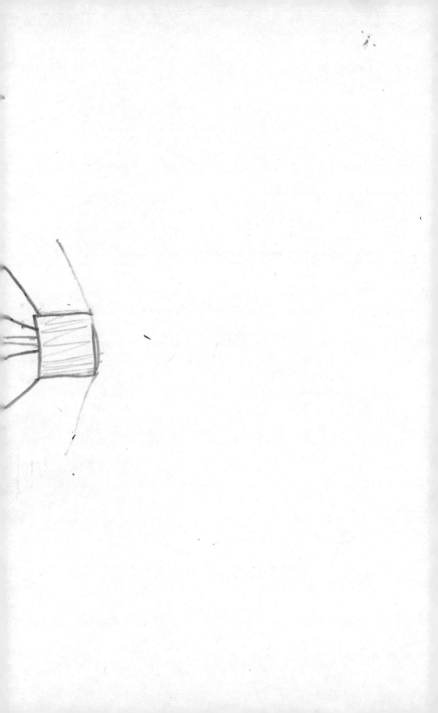

Cigarette from Match

THIS is a very neat way of producing a cigarette and, when properly mastered, can be shown impromptu on many occasions. In effect, the magician shows his audience a match which he holds upright in his right hand between the thumb and forefinger. He then slides his left hand slowly downwards over the match, but instead of the match emerging as his hand descends, a cigarette appears instead.

The cigarette is concealed behind the right hand, nipped in between the first and second fingers. It does not project straight out from the back of the fingers, but lies flat, almost parallel to the back of the hand.

As the left hand is passed downwards over the match, the right fingers are curved inwards, bringing the cigarette forward and into the palm of the left hand. The left hand grasps it and the right hand pushes it upwards into view of the audience. The match is released and drops into the right hand. While the cigarette is being exhibited, the match is quietly placed behind some object on the magician's table.

The Suspended Cigarette

THE performer borrows a cigarette from a member of the audience and passing his hands over it to give it magic properties, places it on the edge of a table with well over half its length projecting beyond the edge. To all appearances, it will fall to the ground, as soon as the magician removes his hand, but when he does take his hand away, the cigarette remains in its place, apparently suspended by some invisible power.

As with a number of other "magnetic" or "anti-gravity" tricks, this effect is accomplished by means of a little moisture. Wet your finger and moisten the tip of the cigarette, being sure to moisten one side only, so the water will not spread and come into sight of the audience. Press the moistened side against the table and the cigarette will stay in place.

The Magician as Salamander

As is well-known, salamanders are supposed to be impervious to fire. In this trick the magician acquires this quality, and extinguishes a burning cigarette in his closed hand.

The left hand is doubled up into a fist and into it a cigarette is pushed with the lighted end first. Instead of wincing at the pain, the magician calmly squeezes his hand more tightly around the cigarette in order to put it out, and then opens his hand to show that he has not been burned at all.

The trick is done by concealing a thimble in the left hand. The lighted end of the cigarette is pushed firmly into the thimble and extinguished in a second or two.

The only hard part of the trick is getting rid of the thimble. This can be done, without the need of any great dexterity, however, by squeezing the left hand with the right, holding the right hand so its palm is upward. This action can be explained by saying the extra pressure is needed to put out the cigarette. As soon as the performer is sure the cigarette is extinguished, he merely relaxes his left hand and allows the thimble to drop into his right palm, immediately afterwards opening up his left hand to show that he is uninjured. The right hand drops the thimble behind some object on the table, or deposits it in a convenient pocket.

The Lengthened Cigarette

IN this trick, the magician takes an ordinary cigarette, one end in each hand, and by pulling it gently, is able to draw it out to twice its normal length.

There is needed, for this trick, one of the long cigarettes which are now obtainable at many tobacco stores. This cigarette is concealed in the left hand, prior to showing the trick. One end is gripped between the thumb and the palm of the hand and the cigarette extends down to the wrist. If the back of the hand is kept towards the audience, the presence of the cigarette cannot be detected.

The normal-size cigarette is taken between the fingers of both hands, which approach each other and then withdraw several times, sliding over the cigarette. The third or fourth time the fingers approach each other, the small cigarette is pushed into the right hand where it is gripped between the thumb and the palm of the hand. At the same moment, the left thumb edges the long cigarette up towards the fingertips and the right fingers seize it and commence to pull upon it. The hands are slowly pulled apart and the cigarette appears to stretch to twice its normal size.

When its full length is revealed, it is taken in the left hand and the performer exhibits it, turning his left side to the audience. The small cigarette is dropped in the right-hand coat pocket.

Cigarette Magnetism

THE magician places a cigarette on the edge of a table, having sufficient of it project beyond the edge so that the cigarette is practically balancing. Taking another cigarette, he holds it about six inches below the one on the table. Explaining that a magnetic current runs between the two cigarettes, he shows that this is true, for as he moves the lower cigarette up and down, the one on the table tips towards it and at length is pulled right off the table, where it drops into the magician's hand.

This would appear to be a trick involving a piece of thread run between the two cigarettes, but in reality the method is much simpler. All the magician does is to blow gently on the projecting end of the cigarette on the table. With a little practice, it can be made to tip as often as one pleases, before falling off to join the other cigarette.

Mysterious Cigar Band

THIS is an effective pocket trick which, when neatly executed, is quite mystifying. The magician exhibits a cigar complete with its band. Presto! The band disappears. In a twinkling, it comes back again, only to disappear again if the magician wishes it to.

The cigar band is one that has been cut in half and pasted onto a cigar. One side of the cigar thus appears banded, though the other side is unbanded. The cigar is held between the right thumb and forefinger with the band side showing. The hand is waved in the air, and at the same time the cigar is turned so that the unbanded side comes into view. The slight turning movement of the cigar is absolutely undetectable, after the motion has been practised carefully.

The Balancing Cigar

WITH careful handling and a bit of showmanship this little trick can be made to appear very mysterious. It consists simply of balancing a cigar on a hat, but if the magician makes it appear as though a thread were used as a support, he can conceal the real method and mislead his audience nicely.

The trick is done with the aid of a pin. It is pushed through the crown of the hat from the inside. The cigar is pushed down on the pin which holds it in an upright position.

The trick can be done equally well with a pencil which has a rubber eraser, the pin in this case entering the rubber.

Mind-reading and Spirit Tricks

The Sealed Message

A SMALL pad is given to one of the spectators with the request that he write on it a name or a date. When he has done so, the paper is placed in an envelop which is sealed. The magician holds the envelop against his forehead for a moment and, by the aid of X-ray vision

or the friendly spirits, he reads what is written on the paper.

The envelop is prepared by cutting a flap in its front side. Care is taken to keep this side downwards throughout the performance. The paper is handed to the magician with the writing on the under side and is put into the envelop the same way. This naturally brings the writing against the face of the envelop. When the envelop is raised to the forehead, the magician simply lifts up the flap with this thumb and he can then see what is written on the paper.

Alarm-clock Mind-reading

THE performer produces an alarm clock and hands it to one of the audience, with the request he set the minute-hand at any number he wishes. While this is being done, the magician turns his back. After the clock has been set the spectator is asked to place it, with his own hands, face downwards on the table. The magician then turns around and, by means of his occult X-ray powers of sight, sees right through the clock and announces the number at which the minute-hand was set to point.

The trick is done by preparing the alarm clock as follows. First set the minute-hand to point at twelve. Then turn the clock over and, with the point of a knife blade, make a small scratch on the winding stem. The scratch should point exactly straight up to the top of the clock. Now when the minute hand is set to point at a number on the face of the clock, the scratch will tell at once where the hand points. Be sure to remember, however, that the imaginary dial on the back of the clock is just the opposite of the dial on the face. Starting at twelve and going from left to right, or clockwise, the numbers read eleven, ten, nine, and so on.

Mind-reading with Cards

THIS is one of the most startling of all mind-reading effects and its execution is simplicity itself. It is carried out chiefly by means of the "pass" described at the beginning of this section.

When presenting the trick, the performer introduces his assistant, who is announced, naturally, as the world's greatest mind-reader and is seated in a chair facing the audience. The magician then asks one of the spectators to choose a card, memorize it, and return it to the pack. Within a few seconds, and with no word being spoken by the performer to his assistant, the latter reads the spectator's mind and announces the name of the chosen card.

The effectiveness of this trick lies to a large extent in the fact that there is no spoken communication whatever between the performer and his assistant. It is accomplished simply by bringing the chosen card to the top of the pack and then slipping it around to the bottom. The pack is then held with the bottom card toward the assistant, who glances at it and a moment or two later reveals its name. The assistant should be warned not to look intently at the bottom card, but to look at it casually when raising his eyes to gaze at the audience.

Book Mind-reading

THIS is a "mind-reading" act that will mystify any audience. Provided you have an assistant with you who knows the secret, it can be performed at a moment's notice at a party or other gathering where you are requested to show your magic skill.

The mind-reader's assistant is blindfolded and seated on a chair and the performer then carries a book to the spectators and asks one of them to insert a card in it at any place he desires. The book is then opened at the page at which the card was inserted, and the mind-reader asks his assistant to tell the number of the page and to read the first line of print. After a few moments of deep concentration, the assistant succeeds in carrying out this well-nigh impossible feat.

The trick is done as follows. Prior to the performance, the mind-reader and his assistant select a certain page in the book that is to be used. The assistant memorizes the page number and the first line. A small white card, similar to the one that is later given to the spectator, is then inserted at this page.

When presenting the trick, the performer holds the book so his card is on the end nearest his body and so invisible to the audience. The spectator then inserts the card given to him. When he has done so, the performer turns away for a moment and faces his assistant, at the same time turning the book around so his card is toward the audience. Now, of course, when the spectator opens the book to the page indicated by the card, it will be the page previously selected by the mind-reader and his assistant.

Who Took the Coin?

THIS trick, if well presented, is sufficient by itself to gain one an enviable reputation as a mind-reader. The effect is as follows:

The performer places a coin and a drinking glass on the table. He then leaves the room, and while he is gone, one of the spectators picks up the coin and puts it in his pocket. The performer then returns and asks each of the spectators to touch "the mystic glass" with his forefinger. After every one has touched the glass, the performer places his forefinger upon it. The vibrations of the glass immediately tell him which of the spectators has the hidden coin.

This capital trick is done with the aid of a confederate. After the performer returns to the room, the confederate watches until the person who picked up the coin touches the glass. The confederate then touches the glass directly after this person, and so reveals to the mind-reader the identity of the one who has the coin.

Second-sight Time Telling

THE magician borrows a watch, or produces one of his own, and asks a spectator to set it at any time he wishes. The only restriction is that the minute-hand is to be pointed towards one of the numerals marked on the dial, such as one, two, five, seven, or nine. The magician leaves the room while the watch is being set and it is then laid face down on the table. Upon returning, however, the magician at once tells at what time the watch has been set.

The trick requires a confederate and a code to designate the hour and minute which has been chosen. The magician and his confederate divide the table into twelve squares, one for each hour. When the watch has been set, the confederate contrives to move it to the required square, either placing it there himself, or else picking it up as if to verify the time and then replacing it in the proper square.

The number of minutes after the hour is indicated by the stem of the watch. The confederate sees to it, that is, that the stem points towards the proper minute. The top of the table represents twelve; a slight inclination to the right indicates five minutes after, and so on around the clock.

The Spirits' Match Box

HERE is a new method of mind-reading which can always be relied upon to interest and puzzle an audience.

The audience writes questions upon small pieces of paper which are carefully folded over. One at a time,

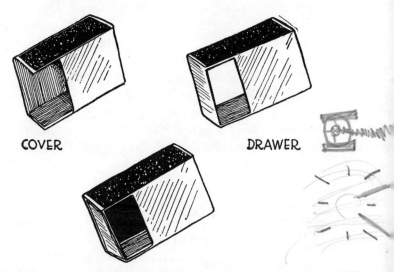

COVER   DRAWER

the papers are put in the spirits' match box, which the performer closes and holds against his forehead. After a few moments' concentration, he reads the question and gives an answer to it. The paper is then removed from the match box and the next one is put in it, the questions and answers continuing as long as desired.

The match box is prepared by cutting away the bottom for about one-third the length of the box. One end of the bottom of the drawer is also cut away in the same manner.

When doing the trick, the magician seats himself at a table having a cloth over it which hangs down far enough to hide his lap from the audience. As soon as a question is put in the match box, he shakes it out into his left hand, which carries it to his lap, where the paper is unfolded and the question read. During this operation, the right hand is holding the match box against the forehead and shading the eyes, so they can look downwards unobserved.

After the question has been read, the paper is refolded. While the magician, with eyes closed, gives an answer to the question, he drops his right hand holding the match box, down to the table's edge, and inserts the paper in the box through the hole in the bottom.

Spirit Messages

HERE is the stand-by effect of the so-called "psychics" for years past. Making the spirits write messages on slates has always been one of their favorite demonstrations, and the method of producing the messages, which is here described, has been used to deceive and mystify hundreds of thousands of people.

The performer shows his audience two slates, exhibiting both sides to prove that nothing is written on them. Placing the slates together, face to face, the magician calls on the spirits to take their customary piece of chalk and write some messages. When the plates are separated, there is a message written on each of them.

The secret of the trick lies in the use of a cardboard

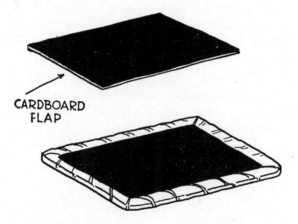

CARDBOARD
FLAP

flap, painted dead black so it looks exactly like the sides of the slates. (It is often a good plan to paint the slates themselves, in order to be sure that they match the flap.) Prior to showing the trick, the magician writes a message on each slate.

The two slates are placed on a table, one with the message side down and the other with the message side up, but covered by the flap.

The covered slate is picked up and shown, front and back. No writing can be seen. It is replaced on the table with the flap side uppermost. The other slate is then placed upon it, with the message side down, and both slates are picked up and turned over. This allows the flap to drop down and cover the message on the second slate. The first slate is then removed and laid on the table with the message side down.

Picking up the second slate, the magician shows it front and back, as the flap covers the writing. It is then placed, flap downwards, on the table. Both slates are now on the table with the messages on their underneath sides. The performer brings them together, with the message sides facing each other. The flap is not picked up, but is left on the table. The performer binds the slates together with a large elastic band, and gives them to a spectator to hold. After calling on the spirits to send some words of wisdom via the slate route, the spectator is requested to remove the rubber band and the messages are revealed.

The Mystic Ashes

THIS is an excellent mind-reading effect that can be performed anywhere without previous preparation. The performer has a small pad and asks each member of the audience to call out the name of some famous person. As the names are given, the performer writes each one down on a separate leaf of the pad, folds the leaf, and drops it into a hat.

When every one has given a name, a member of the audience is asked to draw one of the papers from the hat and to hold it without unfolding it. The performer places the remaining papers in an ash tray and burns them. He fingers the ashes and appears to be concentrating deeply. Finally he states that the name is, say, "Abraham Lincoln." The spectator unfolds his paper and reads aloud the name written on it.

As the "mind-reader" said, the name is "Abraham Lincoln."

The trick is very simply executed. The performer writes on each leaf of the pad the first name called out by a spectator. It then makes no difference which paper is drawn from the hat, for all have the same name written on them.

Red Magic

THE "mind-reader" leaves the room and while he is gone, the audience selects some object—a lamp, chair, table, book, or anything else. When the "mind-reader" returns, his assistant touches various objects, each time asking if it is the one that was selected. The performer says "No!" until the assistant touches the chosen object. Immediately this occurs, he says "Yes, that is it."

The article chosen by the audience is the one the assistant touches immediately after touching some other object that is red—a book bound in red covers, a sofa cushion, a picture with red in it, or anything else that will give the "mind-reader" a definite clue. Though simple, this effect can mystify an audience absolutely.

Naming a Chosen Number

WHILE the "mind-reader" leaves the room, the audience decides upon some number between one and ten. This number, it is explained, will be conveyed to the performer by mental vibrations given off by his assistant. When the performer returns, the assistant seats himself and the performer places his hands on the assistant's temples. Neither of them speaks a word, but both concentrate deeply and in a few moments the performer announces the number that was chosen.

The assistant transmits the number by clinching his jaw the required number of times. This action, which is invisible to the audience, moves certain bones in the temples and the "mind-reader" is able to feel these movements without difficulty.

Which Card?

TWELVE cards are dealt out in a row on the table and the "mind-reader" leaves the room while the audience selects one of them. When the performer returns,

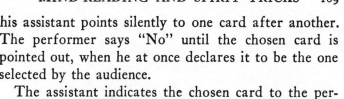

his assistant points silently to one card after another. The performer says "No" until the chosen card is pointed out, when he at once declares it to be the one selected by the audience.

The assistant indicates the chosen card to the performer by pointing to it immediately after he has pointed to one of the cards which is next to either end of the row.

Parlor Mind-reading

SINCE most people believe that in mind-reading tricks, where a blindfolded "medium" is used, the objects which he is to name are communicated to him by some spoken code, it is always useful to have a mind-reading effect which does not depend on this method.

In the present trick, the "medium" is blindfolded and seated in a chair, and the performer asks the audience to choose different objects, either in the room, such as books, pictures, ash trays, etc., or which they have on their persons, such as watches, pins, coins, rings, and so on.

When the various objects have been selected, the performer simply touches them with his hand, never saying a word, and the "medium" at once tells what the objects are.

Before doing the trick, the performer and his "medium" arrange a list of ten or twelve common objects, which each one memorizes. Such a list might be as follows:

Ring	Pin
Book	Ash tray
Watch	Magazine
Vase	Table
Match box	Chair
Coin	Lamp

In any group of people, these objects are bound to be chosen, particularly if the magician suggests the type of object he wishes selected. When all is ready, he starts touching the different objects in the order in which they appear on the list, starting with a ring, then a book, then a watch, and so on.

If the audience fails to choose all the articles on the list, the performer can touch them, anyway, as their turn comes on the list, indicating that this is done to make it harder for the "medium."

Sometimes, two objects of the same type will be chosen and the procedure is then to name them one after the other, the performer indicating this to the medium by some prearranged signal such as saying "Correct" or "Right" after the first object has been named.

If an object is chosen which is not on the list, the best thing to do is to leave it out altogether and, after running through the prearranged list, tell the audience that the effort of concentrating has made the "medium" too tired to continue the experiment any further.

Dollar-bill Mind-reading

THIS simply executed mind-reading trick is very baffling. It is an excellent impromptu trick to remember when you are suddenly called upon to "do some magic," for it requires no preparation.

A dollar bill is borrowed and a spectator is asked to look at its serial number and note whether it is odd or even. He is then asked to cover the number with his fingers and concentrate on the number. The magician very shortly reads the spectator's mind and tells him whether the number is an odd one or an even one.

The trick is done by glancing at the single letter which appears on the face of the bill. If this letter is A, C, E, or G, the serial number will be odd. If the letter is B, D, F, or H, the serial number will be even

Tricks with Numbers

Magic Addition

THIS is one of the best of the number tricks. The audience is given a pad and the performer asks them to write down two rows of figures, each row containing five figures. The performer writes a five-figure number beneath the first two. The audience then writes another figure, and the performer adds still another.

When this has been done, the performer writes something on a piece of paper, folds it, and hands it to a spectator to hold. The five figures written down are then added. The total is, say, 224,354. The spectator is asked to unfold the paper given him and to read aloud what is written on it. He does so and reads the sum of the five figures—224,354!

The trick is done as follows. When the performer writes the third and fifth numbers, he puts down figures that, when added to those just above them, will make a total of 9. Thus, if the second number written by the audience were 36725, the performer would write beneath it 63274. The first numbers of each figure, 3 and 6, total 9, and so do all the others.

The total of the five figures can always be determined in advance by subtracting 2 from the right-hand figure of the first line and placing a 2 in front of the first figure of the first line.

The following example shows how the trick works out:

Audience writes 24356
Audience writes 36725
Performer writes 63274
Audience writes 45328
Performer writes 54671
_____
Total 224354

To Tell a Number Thought of by a Spectator

Ask one of the spectators to think of a number. Tell him to subtract 1 from it, multiply the remainder by 2, and add the number thought of to the product. When he tells you the figure thus arrived at, add 3 to it and divide the resulting number by 3. This will give you the number that was originally thought of.

For example, let us assume that 15 is the number thought of. The spectator subtracts 1 from it and gets 14. He multiplies 14 by 2 and gets 28. Then he adds the original number, 15, to 28 and gets 43. The performer adds 3 to 43, which makes 46. This is not exactly divisible by 3, so the performer divides 3 into the next closest number, or 45. This gives him 15, which was the number thought of.

The Magic Square

THIS is without question one of the best of all mathematical tricks. A little study is required to master it, but it is well worth-while, for the effect is extremely spectacular.

A piece of paper, or cardboard, marked out into twenty-five squares, is exhibited. The mental mathematician asks his audience to select any number between 65 and 500. When a number has been chosen, he proceeds to fill in the squares with numbers that, when added in any direction, vertically, horizontally, or diagonally, total up the chosen number.

The basis of the trick is essentially the key, or number one, magic square. This is shown in the diagram. The numbers in its rows add up to 65 in every direction.

The method by which this square is built up must be understood thoroughly. First, imagine that it is the center square of a group of nine similar squares.

Start filling in the numbers by placing the number 1 in the center square of the top row. The next number, 2, is placed in the square diagonally upwards to the right (see diagram). This places the number 2 in one of the imaginary adjoining squares, but it is brought back into the key square by bringing it down to the bottom row of the key square.

Continue in the same way, placing 3 in the square diagonally upwards and to the right of 2. Number 4 is forced out of the key square, and is consequently brought back in by moving it to the left hand square of the corresponding row of the key square.

The rest of the numbers are filled in by following these two rules, always moving upwards and to the

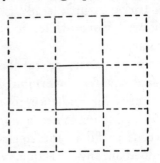

17	24	1	8	15
23	5	7	14	16
4	6	13	20	22
10	12	19	21	3
11	18	25	2	9

	18	25	2	9	
17	24	1	8	15	17
23	5	7	14	16	23
4	6	13	20	22	4
10	12	19	21	3	10
11	18	25	2	9	

right and bringing the numbers back into the key square as described.

There is one more rule. When it is impossible to put a number in the diagonally upwards square, because another number is already there, place the number in the square immediately below the number it is to follow. Thus, 6 is placed below 5, because the regular square is already filled by number 1.

When the key square has been built, memorize the position of five "code" squares, those containing the numbers 17, 7, 22, 12, and 2.

First, the audience select a number.

If it is number 65, the key square provides the answer.

If it is number 66, 67, 68, or 69, the correct square is made by adding 1, 2, 3, or 4 to the numbers in each of the five code squares. Thus, if 66 were chosen, the numbers in the code squares would be 18, 8, 23, 13, and 3.

If the chosen number is 70, or over, use the following rule: subtract 60 from it and divide the remainder by 5. The resulting number is the one to start building the square with. It is placed in the center square of the top row (where number 1 is placed in the key square), and the square is then built up as explained before.

Assume that 150 is chosen. Subtract 60, leaving 90. Divide by 5. This gives you 18. Place 18 in the center square of the top row and build up from it, continuing with 19, 20, 21, and so on.

If a number is chosen which is not divisible by 5, there is another rule to be remembered. Suppose that 327 is selected. Subtract 60, leaving 267. Divide by 5, making 53 with 2 left over. Start the square with 53, but when you come to the "code" squares, add 2 to the numbers that would ordinarily go in them.

Be sure, however, to continue your building from the "code" squares, by using the numbers that would ordinarily have gone into them. In other words, do not continue on from the larger numbers created by adding 2.

Picking the Chosen Digit

TAKING a piece of note-paper the magician writes on it the nine digits, or single numbers, 1, 2, 3, 4, 5, 6, 7, 8, 9. With a mysterious air he then writes something on another piece of paper, folds it, and hands it to a spectator to hold with strict orders not to open it and read what has been written.

Then, by the process described below, the performer makes one of the spectators choose the number 5. When the paper is unfolded, it is found that the number 5 is written on it.

The reason that number 5 is used is because this number is very often picked out first. In doing the trick, the performer gives a spectator a pencil and asks him to cross out a number. If 5 is crossed out, the paper is opened and read at once.

If some other number, say 3, is crossed out, the performer says, "Very good, we have eliminated one number and have eight left. We will divide these into two groups of four numbers each, 1-2-4-5 and 6-7-8-9." He then asks the spectators to choose one of these groups. If it is the first one (with the number 5 in it) he asks the spectator to choose two of the numbers in the group. If he chooses, say 1 and 2, the performer crosses them out and says, "We now have two numbers left. Chose one of them." If 5 is chosen, the magician asks that the paper be opened and read. If, however, 4 is chosen, the magician crosses it out, leaving 5, the number he has, of course, been aiming at since the beginning.

By this method of elimination, any number can be written on the piece of paper, and the others can be eliminated by the means described. If the trick is repeated several times, it is better to vary the number selected.

Important Dates

THE performer asks a spectator to write down the year of his birth and then the year in which some other important event happened, such as his marriage, his entry into business, his graduation from school or college.

Under these two figures, he is asked to write his age at the end of the year. This is not necessarily his age at the time the trick is being done, but is his age as of the following December 31st. One more figure is required, and that is the number of years that have elapsed since the year in which the important event happened.

While the spectator is adding these figures up, the

magician scribbles a number on a piece of paper, and gives it to another spectator to hold. When the total of the spectator's figures is added, the paper is opened and is found to have the correct total written upon it.

This requires no difficult figuring at all, since the answer will always be double the number of the year in which the trick is done.

An example for the year 1935 follows:

```
Birth year....................1903
Important Event ..............1930
Age .........................  32
Years since important event......  5
                               ———
                        3870 = 2 × 1935
```

Telling the Number Thought of

This is probably the simplest and easiest-to-remember method of discovering by "mental arithmetic" what number a person has thought of.

After some one has thought of a number, tell him to double it, add 10, and divide the total by two. Then ask him for the result, and you can tell the original number thought of by subtracting 5 from the figure he gives you.

An example of how the calculation works out is given below:

Original number 9
Doubled 18
Add 10 28
Divide by 2. 14
Subtract 5
                                        ———
Leaves the original number 9

The Chosen Figure

THE magician writes all the digits with the exception of the figure 8 on a piece of paper, thus making the number 12,345,679. One of the audience is asked to choose any number he likes. When he has done so, the magician asks him to multiply the digit number (12,345,679) by another number which he names. The outcome is surprising, for the result of the multiplication consists entirely of the chosen number!

The trick is done by having the spectator multiply by a figure nine times as great as the chosen figure. For example, if 3 were chosen, the multiplication would be as follows:

             12,345,679
                     27   (9 × 3)
             ——————————
             86 419 753
             246 913 58
             ——————————
             333,333,333

The Number in the Envelop

TAKING a piece of note-paper, the performer writes a number on it, without showing it to the audience, and places it in an envelope, which is sealed. He then asks the members of the audience to call out numbers between 1 and 10 and, as they are announced, he writes them down on the envelop. After a half dozen or so numbers have been written down, the magician draws a line beneath the column and, handing the envelop to one of the spectators, asks him to add them up, and then to open the envelope and read what is written on the paper. The number on the paper is the total of the column of figures!

For a simply executed trick, this one is really baffling. First, decide on a number between 35 and 45, say 42, and write it on the piece of paper destined for the envelop. A number of this size is chosen because if seven or eight single numbers are called out at random, they will usually add up to a total somewhere between these two figures.

Having sealed the paper bearing number 42 in the envelop, proceed to write down the audience's numbers as they are called out, adding them up mentally as you write them down. When your mental total approaches 42, tell the audience that you have enough numbers, and after you write the last number, add another that will bring the total up to 42. This will not be noticed as the two numbers can practically be written with one motion and the line is drawn beneath the column immediately afterwards.

An example of how the trick works is given below:

Audience's numbers:

3
8
7
4
9
6
5 Magician's number
—
42

Counting to One Hundred

THIS is one of the most perplexing of all tricks having to do with numbers and, once the simple technic is mastered, it will always serve to puzzle your friends.

The object is for two people, one of them being the magician, to race each other counting to one hundred, subject to certain rules. The first person is to call out a number between one and ten. The second person then adds another number between one and ten. This is continued until one person or the other is able to add a number which will bring the total up to exactly one hundred.

To be sure to win, you must always be the one to name 89, as no matter what number between one and

10 your opponent adds, it will not bring the total up to one hundred. If, for example, he added the highest number allowed, namely ten, it would make the total 99, and by adding 1, you would make it 100 and win.

It is well to bear in mind the figure 78 as well, for by naming this figure, you can always make 89 your own as well. If the precaution regarding naming 78 is not taken, it is sometimes possible for the other person to hit on 89.

Miscellaneous Tricks

The Appearing Flower

THIS is a very surprising trick which is most effective when used to open a magic performance. The magician steps forward and calls attention to the buttonhole in the lapel of his coat. It is empty. He waves his hand over it and immediately a flower appears.

The flower is an artificial one with a piece of elastic cord tide around its stem. The elastic is passed through the buttonhole from front to back and is led down to the next buttonhole where its free end is made fast. The flower is then tucked under the left armpit. In this position the elastic is stretched tight and the moment the left arm is moved slightly outwards to release it, it flashes into place in the lapel. Although its passage is so swift that the flower is practically invisible while in transit, it is well to cover its flight by waving the right hand in front of it.

Burned and Restored Paper

THERE are a number of methods of tearing or other-wise destroying a piece of paper and then restoring it to its original condition, but this one is the best of them.

A long strip of white or pink tissue-paper is exhibited and is then burned either with a match or with the flame of a candle. The performer catches the ashes in his left hand and rubs them together between both hands. After a moment or two, he withdraws the strip of paper perfectly unharmed.

The trick is accomplished with the aid of a duplicate strip of tissue paper. It is pleated into a small square package and is then inserted under a ring worn on the magician's right third finger. It is at the back of the hand and, consequently, the palms can both be shown to be empty.

The original strip is held by the left hand. While it is burning, the performer turns the ring around using his right thumb. This brings the duplicate strip of paper into his right palm, where it is released after the ashes have been rubbed for a few moments.

Changing an Egg to Confetti

THIS is a very beautiful effect, and a very surprising one. The performer shows the audience an egg, which he holds in his right hand. He closes his hand around the egg and waves his hand in the air. A shower of confetti fills the air and falls to the ground. The egg has disappeared.

The trick is done with the aid of a "blown" egg. To prepare it, take an egg and make two small holes, one in each end. Then blow through one of the holes and the contents will be forced out through the opposite hole. One of the holes is then made a little larger and the egg is filled with confetti.

When doing the trick, the right thumb is held over one of the holes and the fingers over the other hole. The hand is then closed over the egg and a gentle pressure will break the shell and release the confetti. The egg-shell will fall down unnoticed, with the confetti.

The Odd Number

THE performer tears a piece of writing-paper into nine square pieces and hands these to different members of the audience. He asks eight of the spectators to write

even numbers on their pieces of paper, but requests the ninth person to write an odd number. The slips are then folded and placed in a hat or on a table. When this has been done, the performer steps forward and immediately picks out the slip containing the odd number.

The trick is done by giving the ninth person the piece of paper that formed the center of the original paper. This piece will be the only one that is torn on all four sides, and can consequently be identified at a glance.

The Pillars of Solomon

THIS is a new and very much improved version of the old Pillars of Solomon trick. In the old trick there were two small pillars of wood with holes bored through them near one end. A piece of string passed through the holes. The string was apparently cut, and the ends of the pillars were separated to show the severed ends of the string. The pillars were then placed together again and the string, apparently restored, was pulled back and forth through the holes in the pillars.

This trick is now known to virtually everybody. The drawing shows how it is done. The string does not pass directly from hole to hole, but runs down through one pillar, through a hole in its bottom to a similar hole in the other pillar, and thence up through the pillar to the hole near the top. Thus, the string is not cut at all, as it is safe out of harm's way all the time.

The new version of this trick is much more bewildering and its secret is not widely known. The apparatus needed can, moreover, easily be made at home. In the

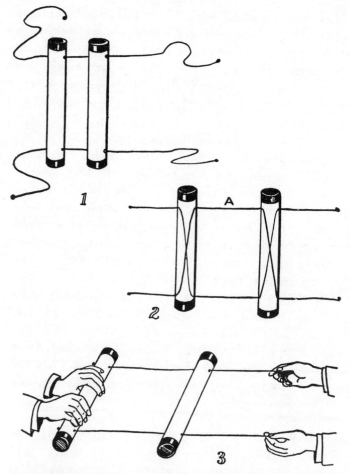

new version, pieces of string pass through both ends of the pillars. The ends of the strings are knotted so they will not slip through the holes.

In showing the trick, the performer asks one member

of the audience to hold one of the pillars, and another member to hold the ends of the strings passing through the other pillar. How this is done is shown in Fig. 3. The performer slides the free pillar along the strings, and then brings both pillars together in the center of the strings. Apparently everything is open and aboveboard.

The performer now asks the audience to choose one of the strings. This is done, and the chosen string is cut —really cut—between the two pillars. The severed ends are shown, and the two pillars are placed together again. The performer pulls on the cut string and it runs through the pillars as at the beginning. The severed ends can be shown as often as desired. Always, however, the string is pulled through the pillars as soon as they are brought together.

The pillars for this trick are made of two pieces of mailing tube, each about eight inches long and one inch in diameter. Holes are punched in them at each end, and the two pieces of string are threaded through them as shown in Fig. 2. The ends of the tubes should be covered with shiny black paper, after the strings have been arranged.

The trick is concluded in a very surprising manner which will convince the most skeptical audience that the cut string has really been restored. The performer cuts away the knot from one end of the string that has been cut. Say, for example, it is the upper string, A, shown in the drawing. One of the audience is then asked to take hold of the knot at the other end of string A, and to pull on it. He does so, and the cut string passes right through both pillars. It is unharmed in any way, and its condition proves beyond doubt that it has been magically restored.

The Reversing Pencil

THE magician shows the audience a pencil and a paper cylinder, or tube, just large enough to fit closely around the pencil. He pushes the pencil into the tube, the blunt

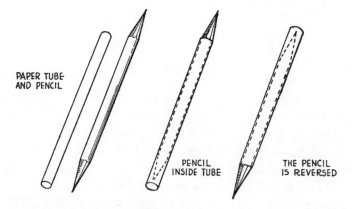

PAPER TUBE AND PENCIL

PENCIL INSIDE TUBE

THE PENCIL IS REVERSED

or unsharpened end going in first. As the pencil emerges from the other end of the tube, it is seen that, in some mysterious way it has reversed itself, for it comes out with the sharpened end first.

This is an exceptionally mystifying trick and is easily prepared. A pencil is sharpened at both ends and is then rolled up in a piece of glazed paper of the same color as the pencil. The paper is glued smoothly in place. It should be of such a length that it just covers one of the sharpened ends, but leaves the other end in view.

When the pencil is pushed into the paper tube, the fingers grip it so the glazed paper covering will remain stationary while the pencil is pushed through it far enough for the hidden pointed end to come out into view. This end will then emerge first from the tube and it will appear as though the pencil had turned around while passing through the tube.

The Magnetized Pencil

THE magician takes a pencil from his pocket and lays it across the back of his left fingers. The hand is then tilted from side to side but the pencil has been magnetized by magical methods and adheres firmly to the fingers until the magician chooses to release it.

The secret lies in the use of a loop of black thread which is fastened to the upper button of the magician's vest. The pencil is passed through the loop just before it is laid across the fingers. The two sides of the loop of thread are passed between the little and third fingers and the second and first fingers. Then, by extending the arm just far enough to stretch the thread to its full length, the pencil can be made to stay firmly in place no matter in what direction the hand is turned.

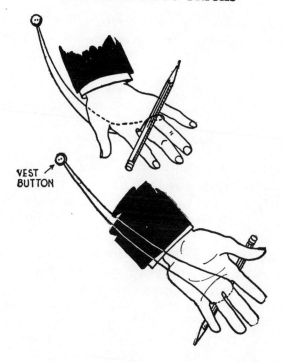

VEST
BUTTON

Pencil and Paper

TAKING a pencil from his pocket, the magician rolls it up in a piece of paper. With a wave of his hand, he commands "Presto! Begone!" The paper is torn in two and the pencil has disappeared completely!

The pencil used in this trick is a fake, made out of glazed colored paper. The sharpened point of a real pencil is glued in one end and an eraser in the other. If the imitation pencil is made carefully, it will look exactly like a real pencil, and can even be used for writing.

The Chinese Blocks

THE apparatus needed for this "stage" trick can easily be made at home. The little time and effort spent in preparing it will be well spent, for the illusion is a very baffling one, and its secret has been closely guarded.

The effect of the trick is as follows. The performer picks up from his table two square wooden blocks which are threaded on a piece of string. He draws the string to and fro several times and then covers the blocks with a handkerchief. He then exhibits a large bead and places the hand holding the bead beneath the handkerchief. Presto! The handkerchief is lifted, and the bead is discovered threaded on the string between the two blocks!

The secret of the trick is made clear by the accompanying drawings. Two beads, exactly alike, are used. One of them is threaded on the string between the two blocks all the time. When the blocks are first shown to the audience, however, this bead is drawn out behind the blocks, as shown, and is concealed within the performer's hand. The string can now be pulled to and fro as often as desired.

The handkerchief placed over the blocks has a hole cut in its center. The string is passed through this hole, and the handkerchief falls down over the blocks and completely conceals them from view. When the performer places his hand holding the duplicate bead beneath the handkerchief, he palms the bead between his

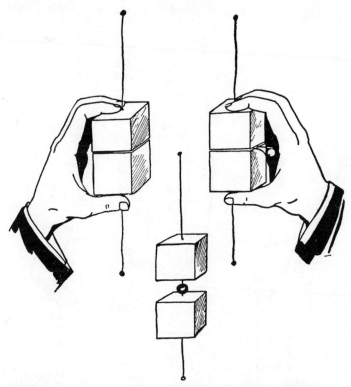

thumb and the base of his forefinger. As soon as he withdraws his hand, he removes the handkerchief, or asks one of the spectators to do so. While every one is gazing at the bead between the blocks, the performer quietly slips the duplicate bead into one of his pockets.

The Bewitched Paper Bands

THE magician exhibits a large loop, or band, made of
newspaper. He cuts it along its center line with a pair

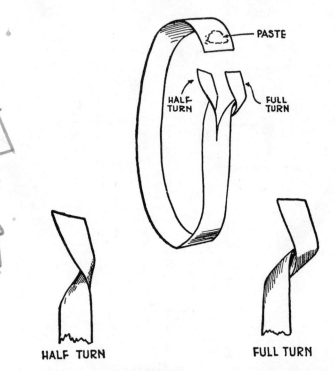

HALF TURN   FULL TURN

of scissors and thus makes two narrower loops. One of
these is cut in two along its center line. Instead of the
two resulting loops being separate, they are linked together! The remaining loop is then treated in the same

manner. It resolves itself, not into two loops, but into a single large loop, twice as large as the original one.

The secret of the trick lies in the preparation of the original loop. This is made from a piece of newspaper measuring four feet in length and four inches in width. To make it the proper length, paste two pieces of newspaper together.

Now cut a slit six inches long in one end of the paper. Cover the uncut end with paste. Take one side of the cut end and bring it to the pasted end; but before pasting it, give the paper a half turn. Take the other side and, before pasting it, give it a full turn. The drawing shows how this is done.

When presenting the trick, the original loop is cut along its center line. The loop in which the paper has been given a full turn is then cut along its center line and produces two linked loops. When the loop containing the half turn is cut, a single large loop is the result.

The Confetti Glass

THIS is a stage trick which is performed by many professional magicians. The apparatus needed for its execution can very easily be made at home, however, and when completed, the trick will be one of the best in your repertoire.

The effect of the trick is as follows. A glass is filled with confetti and is then covered with a cardboard cylinder. The magician utters a few magic words and removes the cylinder. The confetti has disappeared and the glass found to be full of candy.

The trick is done with the aid of a fake which is shown in the drawing. This consists of a piece of cardboard cut to fit inside the glass. To it is glued confetti.

FAKE

CARDBOARD CYLINDER

It is fitted with a circular cardboard top, and confetti is glued to the top also. The top is cut slightly larger than the top of the glass so it projects about 1/16 of an inch beyond the rim. The cylinder is made from a piece of cardboard which is rolled up into a tube which will fit loosely over the glass that is to be used.

When presenting the trick, place an empty glass on your table, and near-by it place a box half filled with confetti. The fake is also placed in this box. It is filled with candy and is stood upside down inside the box.

The performer takes the glass, dips it into the box, and brings it out filled with confetti. He then pours the confetti back into the box. Again he dips the glass into the box, and this time places it over the fake. The glass, with the fake inside it, is then turned right side up and removed from the box. Any loose confetti on top of the fake is brushed off.

The glass is then placed on the table and covered with the cylinder. After the magic words have been spoken, the performer grips the cylinder between his fingers and squeezes it slightly so its sides will press against the projecting top of the fake. He removes the cylinder and the fake comes with it. The glass is revealed full of candy and while the audience are gazing at it, the cylinder and fake are placed out of sight within the box containing the confetti.

The Die in the Handkerchief

FOR this trick a large wooden die measuring about three inches square is needed. This can be made from a square block of wood, or can be purchased at a magic store, for such dies are standard equipment for professional magicians.

The die is passed around the audience and shown to be solid, and is then wrapped up in a large bandana handkerchief. Its form is perfectly outlined and the performer even taps it with his wand to prove that it is there and that it is still solid. Nevertheless, the uttering of a few magic words have their customary effect. The handkerchief is shaken out and the die is found to have disappeared.

The secret of the trick lies in the preparation of the handkerchief which is used. In reality, it consists of two handkerchiefs. They are sewed together around the edges. Between them are placed five square pieces of stout cardboard, each a little larger than one side of

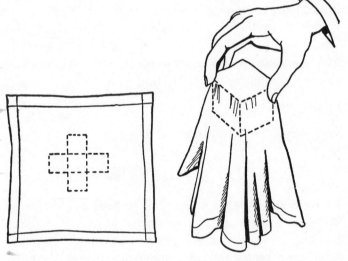

the die. These are arranged as shown by the dotted lines in the illustration. They are joined together with hinges made of tape. The center piece is glued or pasted to one of the handkerchiefs, while the others hang loose upon their hinges.

When presenting the trick, the performer exhibits the solid die and pretends to wrap it up in the handkerchief.

Actually, he keeps it in his hand and, under cover of the folds of the handkerchief, lowers it to the back of his table, placing it behind a box or some other object placed there for this purpose.

The sides of the imitation die between the handkerchiefs fall downward, and it appears exactly as though the solid die were still beneath the handkerchief. Whenever the performer is ready to bring the trick to a conclusion, he shakes out the handkerchief and reveals the instantaneous disappearance of the die.

The Magic Production Tubes

THE magician exhibits to the audience two cardboard tubes which he shows to be empty by holding them up so they can be seen through. The tubes are then placed on the table in an upright position and the magician immediately reaches into them and withdraws dozens of silk handkerchiefs, flags, artificial flowers, and other articles. This is a famous professional illusion which is performed by most of the world's great magicians.

The apparatus required consists of two tubes, numbered 1 and 2, and a piece of wire with a length equal to a little more than one-half the height of the tubes. No. 1 tube should be about twelve inches long and four inches in diameter. No. 2 tube should also be twelve inches long but should have a slightly smaller diameter so it can be passed through No. 1. Both tubes can be made either from mailing tubes or from cylindrical cardboard boxes such as cookies or ice cream are packed in. They should be painted black on the inside, and covered with colored paper on the outside.

The piece of wire is bent, as shown in the drawing, so there is a hook on each end.

To prepare for the trick, the handkerchiefs and other

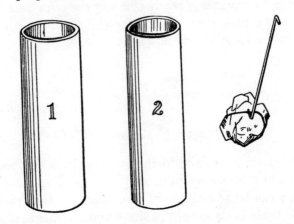

articles which are to be produced are made into a small bundle which is held together by a piece of thread tied around it. One of the ends of the wire is hooked into this bundle, and the other end is then hooked over the upper edge of Tube No. 2. The bundle is thus suspended inside, out of sight. In addition, the performer has in his pocket or on the table, concealed behind some other object, another bundle of half a dozen or more silk handkerchiefs. The handkerchiefs used should be of the type known to magicians as "silks." They can be purchased at magic stores or made at home out of pieces of scrap silk measuring about ten inches square.

In presenting the trick, the performer first shows Tube No. 1 to be empty by holding it up so the audience can see through it. As though further to verify the fact of its emptiness, he passes Tube No. 2 through it. In so doing, he engages the hook on the upper end of the wire on the top edge of Tube No. 1. The wire and bundle thus remain inside Tube No. 1 and Tube No. 2 can be shown to be empty.

About one half of the handkerchiefs and other objects in the bundle in Tube No. 1 are then removed. To do this the performer must, of course, first break the thread surrounding the bundle. Next the performer gets into his right hand the concealed bundle of silks, plunges his hand into Tube No. 2, and withdraws the silks one by one. When they have all been removed, he withdraws the handkerchiefs and other articles still remaining in Tube No. 1.

The wire is removed under cover of one of the handkerchiefs and the tubes are then passed to the audience for examination.

The Thimble Palm

A NUMBER of good tricks can be done with thimbles, many of which depend upon the use of the "thimble palm" here described. It is the method most frequently used by professional magicians to produce a thimble from nowhere or to cause a thimble to disappear into thin air.

To vanish a thimble, it is placed on the tip of the right forefinger. The right hand is then moved toward the left hand and the forefinger is placed within the partially closed left hand. At this moment, the forefinger is bent down to the base of the thumb, and the

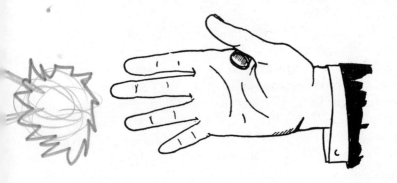

thimble is grasped between the thumb and the base of the forefinger.

The forefinger is then extended and the left hand closes around it and is drawn away as though containing the thimble. A moment later the left hand is opened and shown to be empty, the thimble having disappeared.

To produce a thimble, it is first palmed at the base of the right thumb. The right hand can then be shown quite freely and will appear to be empty. At any moment, the forefinger can be bent down, inserted in the thimble, and then extended, exhibiting the thimble on its tip.

The Multiplying Thimble

THIS trick is done chiefly by means of the "thimble palm" just described. The magician catches four thimbles out of the air, one at a time, and at the end of the trick there is a thimble on the tip of each of the fingers of his right hand.

Prior to doing the trick, the performer secretes three thimbles about his person. One is in the right side of his shirt collar, one in his left vest pocket, and one is placed, mouth downwards, under his belt. A fourth thimble is "thumb-palmed" in the right hand.

The trick is carried out as follows:

The performer catches the thumb-palmed thimble in the air and exhibits it on his right forefinger. He then makes it vanish, by thumb-palming it. Looking about to discover where it has gone to, he puts his forefinger in his shirt collar and brings out the thimble secreted there. This thimble is removed from the forefinger and placed on the middle finger.

The thumb-palmed thimble is then produced and vanished again and is discovered in the vest pocket. It is placed on the fourth finger. Once again the thumb-palmed thimble is caught out of the air and made to disappear. This time it is discovered beneath the performer's belt. It is placed on the little finger. The performer then produces the thumb-palmed thimble from his left elbow and holds up his hand to show each finger crowned with a thimble.

Producing a Thimble from a Paper Cone

THE performer shows a piece of writing-paper, back and front, to the audience and then rolls it up into the shape of a cone, or cornucopia. He shows his right hand to be empty and inserts his right forefinger into the cone. When he withdraws it, there is a thimble on its tip.

The thimble is "thumb-palmed" prior to executing the trick. It is thus well out of sight while the paper is being shown to the audience. When both sides of the paper have been shown, the performer lets go of it with his right hand for an instant and, under cover of the paper, gets the thimble onto his right forefinger. While this is being done, his left hand holds the paper. He then takes hold of the paper again with his right hand, but places his thumb in front and his forefinger behind.

The performer then rolls the paper into a cone shape around the right forefinger. When the cone has been made, the forefinger is withdrawn, leaving the thimble inside.

The Disappearing Thimble

THIS is the easiest method of vanishing a thimble, requiring less sleight of hand than the method generally employed by professionals.

A thimble is placed on a fingertip of the right hand. The left hand removes it. Upon being opened, however, the left hand is empty and the thimble is discovered by the magician in a pocket, behind one of the spectators' ears, or in some other equally suitable place.

This "vanish" is done by a secret substitution of one finger for another. The thimble is placed on the second finger of the right hand, which is extended towards the left, the other fingers being folded in. As the right hand approaches the left, the second finger is tucked in and the forefinger is extended. The forefinger enters the partially closed left hand and is immediately withdrawn. To all appearances, the thimble has been left in the left hand.

With the thimble safely hidden in his right hand, the magician can show his left hand to be empty and can then reproduce the thimble from any place he chooses.

The Thimble Color Change

THIS is a very easy method of performing the famous thimble color change, in which a red thimble is changed into a blue one, right under the spectators' noses, if desired.

The red thimble is put on the tip of the right second finger and, unknown to the audience, the blue one is on the tip of the right forefinger. The second finger with the red thimble is extended, the other fingers being folded in. The right hand moves towards the left and the red thimble is apparently removed by the left hand, closing around the finger, which is withdrawn empty.

Actually, just as the two hands approach each other, the second finger is bent in and the forefinger containing the blue thimble is extended in its place. The left hand closes over it and removes the blue thimble. After a moment the left hand is opened and, instead of the red thimble the audience thought it contained, is shown to hold a blue one.

The Thimble on the Finger

HERE is a very surprising trick which will deceive the most eagle-eyed audience. A thimble is placed on the right forefinger and is covered with a handkerchief. The magician then reaches under the handkerchief and withdraws the thimble, which he replaces on his finger on top of the handkerchief. Thus the handkerchief is beneath the thimble, and between it and the tip of the performer's finger.

With a rapid movement, the performer pulls the handkerchief away. To everybody's astonishment, the thimble stays right on the finger, the handkerchief having apparently passed right through it.

Two thimbles are used, one a little larger than the other. These are fitted together and are placed on the forefinger where they look like a single thimble. After

the handkerchief is placed over the right hand, the per‑
former reaches under it and withdraws the larger
thimble and places it over the finger on top of the hand‑
kerchief.

When whisking the handkerchief away, it is not held
by one corner, but all four corners are gathered up, so
the handkerchief really forms a bag in which the larger
thimble is caught up when the handkerchief is removed.

The Multiplying Corks

MANY of the magic sets sold in the toy stores contain
the old-fashioned version of the "Multiplying Corks"
trick. Three corks are put into a small round box and
are mysteriously increased to six. In the old version, the
three additional corks are glued to the inside of the top
of the box. The box is reversible, that is, the top and
bottom look alike and both can be removed. The multi‑
plication is executed by turning the box upside down
and thus revealing the three secret corks.

There is one disadvantage to this way of doing the
trick, namely, that the three secret corks, being glued
in place, cannot be removed from the box.

An improved method is to attach the secret corks
to the cover with small bits of soap. Then, when the
box is shaken slightly, they will be dislodged and all six
corks can be emptied out onto the table.

The box employed in the trick is a round pill-box,

whose middle section has been separated from the bottom, to which it was originally glued. This makes a reversible box which can be opened either at top or bottom at the magician's pleasure.

Black and Red

THE magician gives the audience a piece of white note-paper to examine and while they are doing so, he builds up a pile of seven checkers. Six of these are red, but the center one is black.

Taking back the paper, he rolls it into a tube which

he places over the checkers. Presto! He removes the tube, and the black checker has disappeared and been replaced by a red one.

The black checker is really a red one around which has been fitted a strip of black paper. While this paper band can be removed when the tube is lifted, by pinching the tube against it, some magicians prefer to make its surface a little sticky by applying a light coating of soap. This causes it to adhere to the inside of the tube and makes its removal easier.

The Five Kings

THIS checker trick is well worth learning, as it will afford your friends a great deal of interest and will puzzle them extremely when they try to duplicate your moves in solving the problem it presents.

The effect is as follows. Ten checkers are laid in a row on the table. The performer then proceeds to make five kings by lifting, one after another, five of the checkers, passing them over the two checkers next to them, and crowning the third checker.

Supposing the checkers to be numbered consecutively 1 to 10 from left to right, the following moves are to be made: Move 4 over 3 and 2 and crown 1; move 6 over 7 and 8 and crown 9; move 8 over 7 and 5 and crown 3; move 2 over 3 and 8 and crown 5; move 10 over 9 and 6 and crown 7.

Locating the Black Checker

A SET of checkers is emptied from its box onto a table and all the red checkers are picked out and placed in a hat. A single black checker is then selected and put in the hat with them. After the checkers have been thoroughly mixed up, the magician puts the hat behind his back and, without the slightest hesitation, produces the one black checker, which is immediately passed for examination to prove that it is not marked in any way that would make it possible to identify it by touch.

The performer prepares for this trick by removing one black checker from the set and either secreting it in his hand or, if he has the opportunity, putting it beneath the band of the hat to be used. This is the black checker that is produced from the hat. After this checker has been produced, the hat is taken from behind the back and the checkers in it are immediately dumped on top of the black checkers which have been left lying on the table, thus concealing the fact that the originally selected black checker was left in the hat all the time.

The Traveling Checker Piles

THE magician shows the audience two piles of checkers, one pile all red, the other all black. Both piles are then wrapped up in pieces of note-paper. The bottom of the paper is even with the bottom of the piles, so the color of the undermost checkers can be seen. The top of the paper extends a few inches above the top of the pile and is twisted around to hold the paper in a cylindrical shape close around the checkers.

The two piles are placed some distance apart on a table and the magician orders them to change places. When the paper covers are removed, it is found that the checkers have obeyed his command.

The trick depends upon two checkers, a red one

colored black on the bottom, and a black one colored red on the bottom. These checkers are placed at the bottom of the two piles, the red one with the other red checkers and the black one at the bottom of the black pile.

When the piles have been encased in paper, the per-

former moves them about on the table, switching them from place to place several times as if undecided just where to put them. During this maneuvering, he turns the bottoms of the two piles toward the audience several times and by this means gets them to believe that the red pile is the black one (since the bottom of the lowest red checker is colored black) and vice versa. When the magician feels sure he has the audience "where he wants them," he places the two piles in their final positions and commands them to change places, which, as can be seen, they do at once.

A Checker Puzzle

WHILE this is not a trick, in the ordinary sense of the word, it is a very interesting puzzle which people will always be interested in trying to solve.

The object of the puzzle is to arrange eight checkers

on a regulation checkerboard in such a manner that no two of the checkers will be in the same line, whether diagonal, horizontal or vertical.

The way to solve the puzzle can be remembered by memorizing the eight figures, 5, 2, 4, 6, 8, 3, 1, and 7. These figures mean that the first checker is to be placed on the *fifth* square of the top row; the next on the *second* square of the row next to the top, and so on.

The Untearable Paper

THE magician shows his audience a large envelop of the type that opens at one end and also a piece of paper cut to such a size and shape as to go into the envelop, leaving a margin of about a quarter of an inch on each side and at the ends.

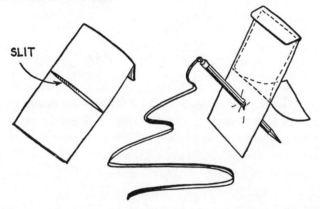

SLIT

The paper is put into the envelop and the magician then takes a penknife and plunges it right through the envelop from side to side. Through the hole made in this way, he then pushes a pencil and a piece of ribbon both of which he proceeds to pull through the envelop and the piece of paper inside it.

To everybody's astonishment, however, the paper is removed from the envelop with no hole or tear in it whatever.

All the preparation needed for this trick is simply to cut a slit across the back of the envelop almost midway of its length. The paper is inserted in the envelop in the regular way, but its entering end is pushed through the slit so as to be outside the envelop. The knife, pencil, and ribbon are, of course, pushed through the end of the envelop which does not have the paper inside it.

Red, White, and Blue

WITH some water-color paints or crayons and four calling-cards, this very startling trick can be easily prepared. It is enough of a "stage trick" to deserve careful practice, since, if done in a finished manner, it will always create a great deal of mystification.

Three small pasteboard cards are shown the audience —one red, one white, and one blue. These are placed in a hat and the magician immediately takes out the red and white cards which he places in one of his pockets. The audience are then asked what is the color of the card remaining in the hat. Naturally, the answer is "Blue"; but the magician turns the hat upside down and out drops the red card. To show that there is no deception, he at once reaches into his pocket and produces the blue and white cards.

The secret lies in the blue card which is colored blue on one side and red on the other. When first shown to the audience, with the red and white cards, care is taken that its blue side alone is seen. When removing

the white and "red" cards from the hat, the magician
really removes the white card and the blue-red one,

showing its red side to the audience. This leaves th
real red card in the hat.

Before doing the trick the performer puts a real blue
card, colored on both sides, in his pocket. Thus, after
dropping the red card out of the hat, he can produce a

genuine blue card from his pocket together with the white one.

The Red, White, and Blue Beads

THE magician shows the audience a small wire ring on which are strung three beads, one red, one white, and one blue. (If you have no wire available, a piece of string will do equally well for the ring.)

The audience, after making sure that it is impossible

to remove the beads from the ring, is asked to choose in what order they would like the beads to be rearranged. Whatever order is chosen, whether white, blue, red; blue, red, white, or any other, the magician, placing the ring behind his back for a moment, produces it with the beads arranged in the desired color formation.

This trick seems impossible of accomplishment, unless the beads are removable, but actually it is done without breaking the ring, or substituting another ring for the original one. A little study will reveal the fact that the beads can be rearranged in any order that the

audience can think of by simply shifting one of the
end beads.

Apart from the original order of red, white, and
blue, there are only five other possible combinations:
red, blue, and white; blue, red, and white; blue, white,
and red; white, red, and blue; and white, blue, and red.
By shifting the red bead around next to the blue one,
you get either white, blue, and red, or red, blue, and
white, according to which side you count from. Blue,
white, and red is, of course, just red, white, and blue
backwards, and the other two combinations are obtained by shifting the blue bead. In spite of its apparent
simplicity, this trick is very puzzling and makes a very
good pocket trick to carry around for impromptu per-
formances.

The Disappearing Spots

In this trick, the magician sits at a table. On the nails
of his two forefingers are stuck two small circles of
black paper. He rests both forefingers on the edge of
the table. Lifting his right hand, he exclaims "Pass"
and immediately lowers his hand, again resting his
finger on the table. The black spot of paper has vanished! The left-hand spot disappears in the same manner, and then both spots are made to reappear.

What really happens is this. When the forefingers
are first rested on the table, the other fingers are kept

closed. To make one of the spots vanish, the hand is raised and just as it is being lowered, the forefinger is doubled back and the second, or middle finger, is extended to take its place. This simple ruse is very difficult to detect, if executed smartly.

To cause the spots to reappear, the middle fingers are closed and the forefingers are extended just before the hands reach the table.

Changing Dice Spots

ONCE the knack of this trick is learned, it will be exceptionally puzzling to the onlookers. They can easily be led to believe that the magician is using a pair of specially prepared dice whose spots are changed by mechanical means.

The trick is simplicity itself. Two dice are held between the right thumb and forefinger. Their upper sides are shown to the audience. The magician blows on them and "Presto," the spots have changed to different ones.

The change is effected by a very slight, but quickly executed, twisting movement of the thumb and fingers. This turns the dice one-quarter of the way around and exposes the sides adjoining those which were first shown to the audience.

The Obedient Watch

THE magician passes a watch around the audience so that all can see that it is running and in good order. Then, with a wave of his hand, he commands it to stop and it does so. It can be started and stopped again as often as is desired.

The secret *modus operandi* is a magnet which the magician keeps concealed in one hand. As soon as the watch is placed against the magnet it will stop running. There is one precaution to be observed when doing this trick and that is not to use a really good watch, as its sensitive mechanism might be harmed. With an old dollar Ingersoll, however, you will always be on safe ground.

Counting the Hours

IN this trick the magician gives some member of the audience a watch and asks him to think of any hour of the twelve. The performer, then, by means of magic, proceeds to divine the chosen hour.

This is done by tapping with a pencil according to a certain method, on the different hours marked on the watch dial. Before beginning the taps, the performer asks the spectator to count them to himself, giving to the first tap the number just following that of the chosen hour, giving the second tap the next highest number, and so on.

Thus, if the spectator thought of two, he would count the first tap as three, the next as four, and so on. When, by this method of counting, he reaches twenty he is to call "Stop." On this tap, the magician's pencil will be resting on the chosen hour.

The first seven taps are made at random. The eighth tap, however, should be on the figure twelve, the ninth on eleven, the tenth on ten, and so on. The trick then works itself and comes out correctly every time.

The Bending Watch

THIS is a most amusing and deceptive effect which is based upon an optical illusion. A watch is borrowed and the performer holds it between his two hands. The thumbs are on the side towards the magician's body; the fingers on the side towards the audience, the watch being held upright, with its back towards the audience.

The hands are now bent outward and at the same moment the fingertips are pushed towards each other. Drawing the hands back to their original position, the fingertips are drawn apart. This movement is repeated several times, and each time it appears as though the watch were being bent backwards and forwards as if it were made of rubber.

The Spools-and-String Trick

THE magician threads three spools onto two pieces of string, held parallel to each other, and gives the ends of the string to two spectators to hold. One of the strings is tied into a knot, apparently making it impos-

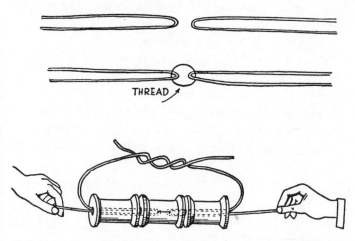

THREAD

sible to remove the spools. The performer, however, throws a handkerchief over the spools, reaches underneath it, and in a moment releases the spools, leaving the strings intact in the spectators' hands.

The strings are prepared before showing the trick. Each piece is doubled back on itself so that it forms a loop, and the two pieces are then tied together, as shown in the illustration, with a single piece of thread. The strings are picked up from the table and one of the spools is threaded onto it in front of the audience, but the magician is careful not to call particular attention to the strings until after this first spool is in place and is covering the join between the two loops of string.

The two other spools are then threaded onto the strings, one on each side of the first spool, and two spectators are asked to hold the ends of the strings. The magician then takes one string from each of the spectators and ties the two ends into a single knot. This gives each spectator an end previously held by the other one, as the ends are crossed in tying the knot.

Now, it is only necessary to throw a handkerchief over the spools, reach under and grasp them firmly in one hand, and tell the spectators to pull sharply on the strings. When they pull, the thread holding the strings together will break, releasing the spools, and leaving the spectators with the strings in their hands.

The Eggs in the Hat

IF you are fond of doing magic for children, this trick is one that will always delight a young audience. The magician borrows, or produces, a derby hat, which he places on the table, with the head opening facing upwards. To prevent possible damage, during the course of the trick, a handkerchief is placed inside the hat.

A large bandana handkerchief is then exhibited and folded once lengthwise. The magician holds it by the two upper corners, shakes it once or twice, and an egg rolls out of it and into the hat. The handkerchief is shaken again and again until half a dozen or more eggs have been dropped into the hat in this mysterious fashion.

When the hat appears to be nearly full, the magician picks it up and, as if by accident, drops it to the floor. Everybody expects the eggs to break, but to their as-

tonishment the hat bounces away and is seen to be empty, all the eggs having vanished.

The trick is done with the aid of a single blown egg (one from which the contents have been blown by punching a small hole in each end). This is fastened by a thread to the edge of the bandana, so the egg hangs as shown in the illustration.

Prior to doing the trick, the handkerchief is laid on the table with the egg out of sight beneath it. The performer picks up the handkerchief so that the egg hangs down on the side towards himself and is thus invisible to the audience. The bottom edge of the handkerchief is then folded up so that it meets the top edge, the egg being concealed within the fold.

Now, the egg can easily be made to roll out of the handkerchief and apparently into the hat. The real purpose of the handkerchief placed inside the hat is to form a cushion which would deaden the sound of a real egg falling into the hat. If it were not there, the audience might become suspicious when they did not hear a thud each time the blown egg is rolled out of the handkerchief.

After the first egg has been rolled into the hat, the handkerchief is spread out in front of the hat and picked up by the two upper corners, the egg hanging down on the side towards the performer. The handkerchief is then folded once again and another egg is produced, this process being repeated as often as the performer desires.

Appearing Chinese Coins

CHINESE coins, with holes through their centers, can be obtained from any stamp-and-coin dealer and are used in this trick, though if they are unobtainable, metal washers can be used in their place.

The magician shows both his hands empty. He then places them together and shakes them up and down. At once the clink of metal is heard and when the hands are opened, there are six Chinese coins in them, which have mysteriously come from nowhere.

The coins were behind the right hand, suspended by a loop of thread around the thumb. The thread passes through the holes in the coins, thus holding them com-

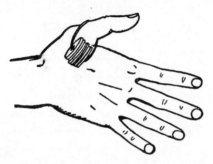

pactly together. When the hands are brought together, the coins are slipped over into the palm of the right hand, the thread is broken, and the coins are revealed to the audience.

If the magician prefers, he can produce the coins in a more spectacular fashion by catching them out of the air. This requires a little practice, as the hand must be turned so the audience cannot see the coins slipping from back to front, but it is not difficult.

Color Changing Spools

THE magician exhibits two spools, one with blue silk thread and the other with red thread. A long piece of string is passed through them; they are covered with a handkerchief, and the ends of the string are given to two spectators to hold. The magician reaches underneath the handkerchief for a moment, tells the spectators to hold tight so nothing can pass off the ends of the string, and, an instant later, removes the handkerchief. The two spools are found to have changed places!

The secret lies in the preparation of the spools prior to the performance. Around the red spool is glued a tight-fitting piece of blue paper; while a piece of red paper is fitted in similar fashion around the blue spool. At a short distance the deception is undetectable.

The magician tears the papers off, using his fingernails, when he reaches under the handkerchief. He retains the papers, crumpled up, in his hand, and removes the handkerchief with the same hand, throwing it on the table with the papers beneath it. The spools and string are then passed for examination.

The Non-wettable Hand

As a demonstration of his power over the elements, the magician commands a bowl of water to become "magicked" in such a way that it will not wet him. He dips his hand into the bowl and withdraws it perfectly dry.

The magic is not in the water, but in the preparation

of the magician's hand. Before doing the trick, he covers it thoroughly with stearate of zinc (obtainable at drug-stores). This is rubbed well in. It is then possible to dip the hand into a bowl of water and bring it out absolutely dry. The only precaution to take is not to keep the hand in the water for more than an instant.

Producing a Glass of Water from a Pocket

WHEN a glass of water is needed for a trick such as, for instance, changing water into ink, the magician can demonstrate his ability to achieve the impossible by reaching into his pocket and taking from it a glass filled with water. The effect is always startling and it is easy to do.

The glass is covered with a piece of rubber, which can either be purchased in sheet form or made out of a child's balloon. The rubber is stretched tight and is held in place by a rubber band encircling the glass.

To guard against any of the water spilling out into the pocket during the process of withdrawing the glass, one hand should take hold of the glass from outside the pocket. The other hand then reaches into the pocket, removes the rubber covering, and draws out the glass.

The Inverted Glass of Water

THE magician fills a glass with water and places a sheet of paper over its mouth. The glass is then turned upside down, but the water remains in the glass. This will appear quite mysterious to most people who do not know that this is a simple experiment in physics. The magician, however, proceeds to carry the experiment a step further by drawing away the piece of paper. Though the glass is still upside down, the water does not flow out.

After a moment or two, the magician holds the glass over a bowl, or pitcher, and upon his uttering the mystic command "Pass," the water is released and pours out into the bowl.

The trick is done with the aid of a circular piece of transparent celluloid cut to fit evenly over the mouth of the glass. It is placed on the table underneath the piece of paper before the commencement of the trick.

The paper should be slightly damp. It is picked up, together with the celluloid, and as it is placed over the mouth of the glass, the celluloid is fitted into place, so it is directly on top of the glass.

When this is done, the glass is turned over, one hand being kept firmly pressed against the paper to keep it from coming free before the inversion is completed.

The paper should be removed slowly so as not to dislodge the celluloid. After the glass has been exhibited full of water upside down, it is placed over the bowl and the celluloid is dislodged by a touch of the finger. It drops into the bowl and the water escapes from the glass which is then passed for examination.

Ruler and Newspaper

THIS is an interesting experiment that has to be seen to be believed. A ruler is placed on the edge of a table so that it projects just enough to balance itself. A newspaper is then spread over the end which rests on the table.

Any one would think that if the projecting end of the ruler were struck downwards, the paper would fly into the air. This is not true, however, for the suction created by the paper keeps it on the table, almost as though it were glued in place.

Changing Ink to Water

THIS is a favorite trick with the children and can always be relied upon to amuse and mystify them. The performer exhibits a glass partly filled with ink and to prove that it is the genuine article, he dips a white card into it. The card emerges with its lower portion colored black by the ink. The glass is then covered with a table

napkin and when it is removed, the ink is gone and the
glass is filled with water.

The ink is really a piece of black cloth sewed into
a cylindrical shape, and just large enough to fit inside
the glass to be used. To it is attached a black thread
with a small button fastened to the free end. The but-

ton hangs over the edge of the glass out of sight behind
the "ink." When the napkin is draped over the glass,
the magician locates the button and in removing the
napkin, pulls the button and black cloth away at the
same time.

The card used to demonstrate the genuineness of the
ink is prepared by inking the lower half of one side. The
unprepared completely white side is first shown the
audience and the card is turned around after it has been

dipped into the glass, so that when it is removed, the audience sees the inked side.

Changing Water to Ink

THIS trick can be worked effectively in conjunction with the preceding one. After the ink has been changed to water, the magician states that he will reverse the process and change the water back to ink.

This is most easily accomplished by dropping into the water one of the regular tablets for making ink which are sold by stationery stores. The tablet is concealed in the folds of a handkerchief, which is draped over the glass during the transformation.

(Boon)